Victor Saunders was born in Lossiemouth and grew up in Malaya. He started climbing in the Alps in 1978 and has climbed in the Caucasus, India, Pakistan, Nepal and Bhutan, including four years in the Karakoram. He is an architect and a member of the North London Mountaineering Club. *Elusive Summits* was the winner of the 1990 Boardman Tasker Prize for mountain literature.

Victor Saunders
ELUSIVE SUMMITS
FOUR EXPEDITIONS IN THE KARAKORAM

SPHERE BOOKS LTD

A *Sphere* Book

First published in Great Britain by Hodder and Stoughton 1990
Published by Sphere Books 1991

FRONT COVER (main picture) the Golden Pillar of Spantik
by Victor Saunders and (inset) Victor Saunders.

ISBN 0 7474 0968 4

Printed and bound in Great Britain by
The Guernsey Press Co. Ltd., Guernsey, Channel Islands.

Sphere Books Ltd
A Division of
Macdonald & Co (Publishers) Ltd
165 Great Dover Street
London SE1 4YA

A member of Maxwell Macmillan Publishing Corporation

For Ben

I should like to thank
Maggie Urmston and
Maggie Body for
making this book
possible.

CONTENTS

MAPS AND DRAWINGS

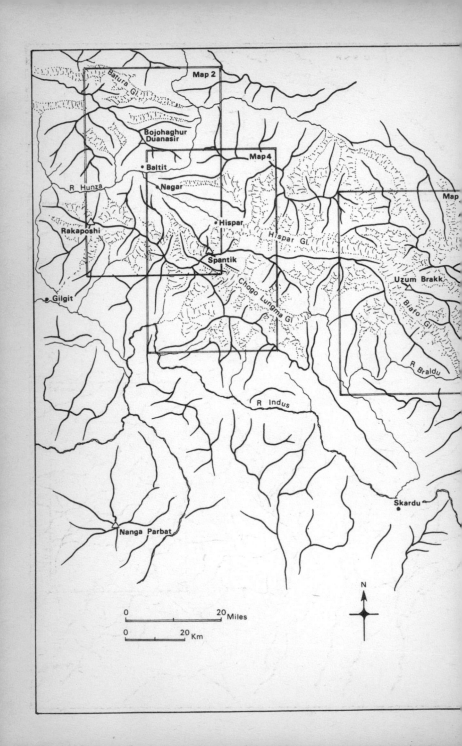

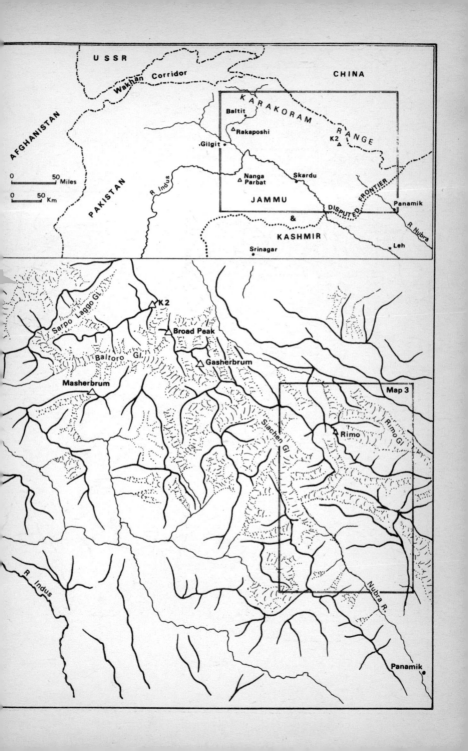

PART ONE

Uzum Brakk, 1980

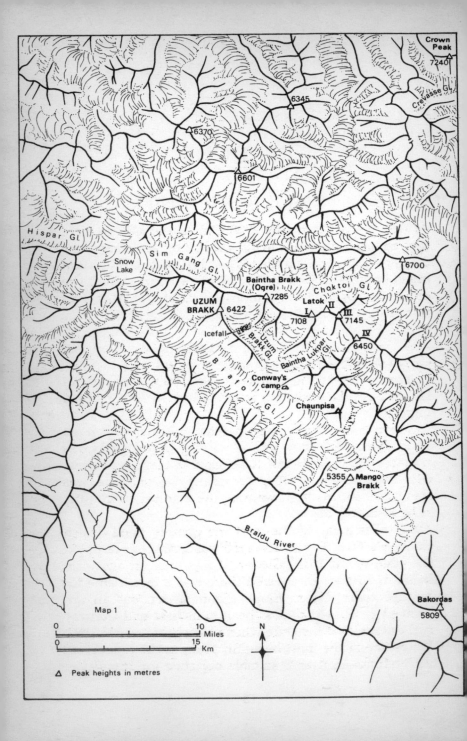

Map 1

0 ——————— 10 Miles
0 ——————— 15 Km

△ Peak heights in metres

1

At 6.00 pm on 18th July 1980 Omiya and Okano were digging a bivouac ledge in a slight hollow, unaware of the danger that hollow implied. They had reached the summit of Latok IV (21,162 ft/6450 m) a few hours earlier. The mountain had not been climbed before, and the pair were rightly pleased. It had been a three-day effort so far, they should be with their friends by Day 4. With flailing ice axes Omiya and Okano dug furiously. It was then that Omiya saw the first sign of their predicament.

"I saw a hole through which the snow was pouring . . . I looked up and the weather was very bad, so we continued digging."

Omiya and Okano were perched over a very large sérac. The slight hollow into which they were digging was no more than a two-foot thick sagging blanket of snow over an awesomely deep crevasse. The outcome was inevitable, and without warning the two men were catapulted into the abyss.

Six miles away to the west the grandly titled British Conway's Ogre Expedition 1980 was setting up camp on the edge of the Biafo Glacier. It was only on arrival in Baltistan that we discovered there was a local name for our mountain, Uzum Brakk. Uzum Brakk was an unclimbed peak. No one had been to its base and Conway had christened it the Ogre when passing this way in 1892. It was one of the most beautiful peaks in the region and we had chosen it as a suitable objective for Himalayan first-timers. Not too high at 21,068 feet (6422 metres), the climbing would be a reasonable extension of our previous Alpine experience. But we had not been prepared for the glaciers.

There were three climbers on our trip. Cairns Dixon, a botanist turned teacher, was the expedition leader. As such he wore a tie most of the time. Both he and Will Tapsfield, the expedition doctor, lived in Edinburgh, though Will did so as an English migrant. And I, a London-based architect, was the only mere expedition member on the official forms. There were a lot of those.

While we were setting up camp, the porters, who had outwitted us by locating the Base lower down the glacier than we intended, showed us how to make stone chapatis by wrapping the dough round egg-sized pebbles, and how to curry bharal (blue sheep) with chive heads. They also gathered the wild rhubarb and ate the flower-heads raw. Next day, after they had left, we walked up the Biafo Glacier to examine the western approaches to Uzum Brakk. Fanny Bullock Workman was here. In the Royal Geographical Society Library I had seen the photograph, her eyes like beads, staring straight into the camera, in the sepia distance, the chain of porters, full length skirt. Will and I went on to explore the eastern approaches to our mountain, while Cairns, still recovering from a mystery illness, stayed in camp. The Biafo Glacier is enormous, Alpine proportions do not apply and the wind made a baleful noise.

While we explored the Biafo, Okano was trying to fight his way out of the crevasse, but it was lens-shaped and where it overhung, he kept falling. He already had three broken ribs, the successive falls aggravated the injury. Omiya was unconscious for twenty-four hours after the accident, blood oozing from his ear. In addition, he had a complex compound fracture of his right tibia. Bits of bone were sticking out of his leg. He could not wear the right boot or crampon. Yet, as Okano's efforts flagged, Omiya resolved to reach the faintest glimmer of light, at the edge of the crevasse. Wearing only the one boot and crampon (the injured foot was cased in the remaining inner boot), Omiya used ice pegs to climb across the side of the coffin in two pitches. He tried to pull Okano through, but Okano was so exhausted by his earlier efforts that he could not follow. Omiya took in the rope to find, to his dismay, that the end was untied. He cut his way through the edge of the crevasse, hobble-climbed to its lower lip and dropped the rope down to Okano, who was in such pain, he was unable to prusik up it.

It was the 22nd. Four days since the accident. Omiya, with no food, or sleeping bag, spent the night out on the ice face.

Will sat near the entrance of our tent heating a panful of slushy snow. Supper time. It was the first bivouac of our expedition, which had got off to a rather groggy start, and now at last Will and I were confronted with our first 'mountaineering' problem, a vast and nasty-looking ice-fall. After two days with twenty-kilo loads, it was not an encouraging sight. We observed the icefall without pleasure. It was a loosely held tumble of séracs, like the spillage from a container full of monstrous sugar cubes. To reach our mountain we would have to pass this obstacle.

Rising very early on the morning of the 23rd, Will and I roped up to inspect a possible route, keeping to the middle to minimise the risk from those tottering, fawlty towers. By 7.30 am, the sun had caught us high on the icefall. In danger from collapsing towers and bridges, we turned back to slither down the ramps and abseil the cliffs.

Meanwhile, beneath Latok IV, Omiya was slowly and painfully down-climbing the icewall below the crevasse in which Okano remained incarcerated. He hobbled on his one good leg, trying to protect the other from sudden movement. The early sun helped to ease the stiffening cold out of his limbs.

Having escaped the icefall just as the sun began to loosen it, Will and I decided to dump our excess baggage here, high up on the Uzum Brakk Glacier. We were proud of our new Gore-tex bivi-bags, having not yet discovered their limitations. Although Will had new-fangled plastic boots, I was still using my double leather Makalus, almost as heavy as diving boots. Crampons, ice axe, duvet, food, all wrapped in a Karrimat for protection, were stuffed inside the two bivi-bags. Then we ran down the Uzum Brakk Glacier to Base, unladen, to get home in time for tea.

Omiya spent the entire day covering 200 yards of difficult steep ground. He had no rope. From Latok IV a pinnacled ridge sweeps down to a 600-foot ice face above the Japanese Camp 2. By late afternoon, Omiya reached the ridge. Unable to shout, he waved desperately at the clutch of tents far below. Omiya and Okano were now three days overdue. The weather had not been too bad to climb in, so the three other members of the Japanese team had become increasingly concerned at Camp 2, though there was not much they could do, being support members and not strong enough mountaineers to investigate higher on the mountain. One of them actually spotted Omiya high on the ridge above waving. Delighted, they waved back, then returned happily to the tent to prepare tea for the returning mountaineers. But Omiya did not arrive, and by nightfall they were aware that something had gone wrong.

Forty-eight years earlier, a similar moment of false reassurance had occurred when, from the safety of a tunnel shaft which opens out onto the North Face of the Eiger, a railway worker had spoken with the Hinterstoisser party as they were descending. He too returned to his stove to make tea. The tea was brewed. He waited an hour, then another, the tea grew cold. He went out again, and found that, of the four climbers he had spoken to, only one remained alive, and he, Toni Kurtz, was badly injured. Kurtz would not survive the following day. Would the cyclic view of climbing history apply on Latok?

Will, Cairns and I had started for a reconnaissance of Uzum Brakk, and were about half an hour across the rubble of the Uzum Brakk Glacier, when we saw two men, our liaison officer and his Japanese expedition counterpart, on the bank of the moraine we had left, shouting and waving. We waved back and turned to go, but they kept on waving and shouting. Across the frozen waves of glacial rubble we caught the word 'accident', and 'crevasse'. Cairns, who was fully equipped, went straight up to the Japanese Camp 2 with the liaison officers. Will and I returned to our Base for spare crampons and axes, then to the Japanese Camp 1, where we dined on seaweed and strips of dried meat of indeterminate origin. The next morning we met Cairns and the three Japanese support climbers on their way down from Camp 2. They were towing what looked like a corpse.

We approached them with heavy hearts. Then the corpse sat up and said, "Herro! How do you doh!" Happily, we helped drag Omiya to Camp 1, where he was propped up against a boulder and began to take over the organisation of his team. "Handa, you make the tea . . . Cook, how much rice is there?" and so on. There was a dull roaring in the background. "Ah!" said Omiya. "Latok I!" even though he had his back to the mountain.

Omiya was built like a bull. He needed to be to survive. As he bossed his team, he explained the exact position of the hole down which Okano was, we hoped, waiting. At midnight the three Brits set off up Latok IV. We climbed a 2000-foot ice face and ridge, avoiding the easier but longer Japanese line. There were no tracks. Would we trace the line of Japanese descent? Would we find the four-foot square hole? Would Okano be alive? Could he be rescued?

Cairns was marginally slower than I who was

considerably slower than Will. But then Will and I had acclimatised by our previous efforts. We climbed in our separate pools of light. Only when the dawn flooded the connective space and we could see each other did we begin to converse. It was as if the darkness had formed a solid barrier between us. Our main concern was Okano's state of mind, should we find him. If he had perished, a mountain burial would pose a few problems. If injured, but fully compos mentis, we could probably escort him, although slowly, to safety. But it was now the 26th, Okano's ninth day of incarceration. The big problem would be insanity. We all knew the story of Bonatti and Mazeaud's terrible descent from the Frêney Pillar in 1961 when one by one the rest of their party died from exhaustion and a delirious Kohlman had attacked his helpers, endangering them all. We had visions of Okano flailing his ice axes madly, while we kept him on a tight rope between us. Should Okano have cracked, it would be difficult to manoeuvre him through the intricate sequence of techniques needed for a safe descent. Not only would it be difficult for him, he would also endanger us. Please, we prayed, let him not be insane, or at least, not too much so.

By 11.00 am we were below a pair of Japanese ice screws, from which a red line led over a lip into a hole in the ice. Will, Cairns and I peered into the hole. It was just four feet across. After 3000 feet of climbing, some of it in the dark, we had climbed straight up to the abyss, as if we had been there before. It must have been Cairns or Will who had the unerring sense of direction. It was certainly not me. In London I cannot find my way home from the pub, even though I live round the corner.

At the bottom of the 120-foot shaft was a patch of colour, some blue and some red. Cairns shouted down. We all shouted. There was no answer, no movement. Cairns looked appalled.

"Oh, God . . . " he said.

"The poor bugger's had it," said Will. Will abseiled

down Omiya's rope, knocking icicles and snowdrift onto the red and blue. "He's not here! These are just a pair of rucksacks."

Will followed a ledge system out of our sight. He was still tied on to the rope and with each movement great chandeliers of ice crashed and tinkled down the crevasse. (It was like a mausoleum, gothic columns of ice, vaulted in the late perpendicular style.)

Will found Okano was lying on a snow ledge surrounded by ice-rimed bivouac equipment – empty packets of food, discarded gas cylinders, frozen sleeping bags. He was not fully conscious. He had not eaten or drunk for three days, not seen light for eight days. Okano was waiting to die . . . he was in limbo.

Cairns and I sent a stove and pan down on the end of our rope and Okano seemed to recover after Will made him drink tea. Then Will tied Okano onto our rope for Cairns and me to haul the poor man up. Will would jumar up behind. Using Yosemite sack-hauling techniques, Cairns and I heaved Okano up the crevasse and over its lip. He looked confused and frightened. I tried to console him with the only Japanese phrase I could remember: *"Konichi wa, Okano San, ie genki des ka?"* [How are you, Mr Okano, are you well?]

Okano looked even more confused and frightened than before. Perhaps I hadn't got it quite right. It took a while, but eventually we made Okano realise he was with friends, and not ghosts. His down jacket and sleeping bag had filled with ice during his incarceration, so we abandoned them, and put my jacket on him. He said nothing but sat, blinking, in the sun, soaking in the feelings of warmth, air, life. Even we could see how released he was.

Meanwhile, we had completely forgotten about Will, who should have followed Okano over the edge, but when Cairns looked down, there he was, at the bottom of the pitch. Around him lay a tangle of slings and rope.

"What . . . is . . . the . . . matter?" Cairns bellowed into the darkness.

"I cannot get the jumars to work!" came the faint reply.

"Are they frozen?"

"I do not think so."

"What . . . is . . . going . . . on?"

"I forgot to tell you," came the faint and plaintive reply, "I've never jumared before."

Cairns raised his eyes heavenward, and turned to me. "Come on, we had better start hauling him up too."

As Cairns and I began to help Will up, Okano fidgeted and gestured, saying something in Japanese and trying to undo his harness.

"Hey! stop that!" Cairns bellowed, but Okano continued to fiddle with the straps. Cairns made a dash for him. "Here, give us a hand!" he shouted to me, while the two of them struggled for control of the buckle on the harness. I dropped Will's rope, which slithered over the edge. There was a distant thud, followed by faint howls of rage from the crevasse. I helped tie Okano up in knots, while Cairns gave him a jolly good talking to about why he wasn't to fiddle with his harness, or undo his belay again.

Okano couldn't speak English, and what we did not know, what we only found out later, at Base Camp, was that the tea had gone straight through. He desperately needed to pee. So by the time we had hauled Will back up to the surface, Okano had become frantic again. When he saw all three of us looking at him, he started pointing, trying to indicate in sign language what he needed.

"He's pointing at his balls now!" said Cairns, who had earlier explained to Will that Okano had been trying to commit suicide, probably because of Japanese loss of face.

"I think he has finally flipped," I added usefully.

"This will calm him down," said Dr Will, producing the phial of Japanese morphiates, and a long-needled syringe. Okano stared at Will in horror, and began to struggle more urgently than ever.

It took both Cairns and me all our strength to hold Okano down, while Will ministered to his needs. Soon Okano became quite peaceful again. But he was wearing my duvet jacket, and for the rest of the expedition there would be a scent of urine from this garment whenever it became damp.

We took stock. It was gone midday. We were at 20,000 feet. We were clearly going to have to spend the night out on the ridge or face, though it was hard to believe the seriousness of our position as we looked out from our ledge. It was a beautiful sight, range on range of Karakoram peaks fading into the distant haze below a cotton-dotted sky. Opposite us a jumble of glaciers plunged between the ice-sheathed spires of the unexplored Chaunpisa massif; broken séracs, dappled silver under the dalmatian sky, fed a broad river of ice beneath us, the Chaunpisa Glacier. If we descended to that glacier, we should at least be on flat ground by nightfall. The problem was that the Japanese camps were on the Baintha Lukpar Glacier, and to reach this we were going to have to climb up to a break in the ridge, and descend a 600-foot icewall, risking a night on a small ice ledge. That alternative was unthinkable. Okano would not survive the bivouac. The Chaunpisa Glacier was a thousand feet below, half a dozen abseils, but Okano was too weak to stand, let alone abseil. At first we tried to climb down the ridge, and after a few faltering steps, Okano collapsed. We helped him up.

"Please try," we said. "It's very important to get down quickly."

"Yes," said Okano, "I understand . . . I understand." It was his one phrase. Then he collapsed again.

"It's hopeless," said Cairns, "we'll never get him down the ridge."

"Our only hope is to get him down to the Chaunpisa before dark. We'll have to abseil."

"Okay," said Cairns, "you abseil down with Okano,

23

Will and I will lower him."

We reached the glacier at dusk, at 18,000 feet it was going to be a cold night. The clouds had drifted over, bringing threats of wind and snow. It was important to keep Okano warm. He was already wearing my duvet jacket. We encased him in Will's sleeping bag, then slid the Okano sausage into a big Gore-tex bag, like a tent without poles. Will and I sat shivering either side of the sausage, making it sit up at regular intervals throughout the night to sip from our communal mug of tea. It took Cairns forty minutes to heat the glacial ice to a drinkable temperature. Poor Okano! Every time he began to fall asleep we shook him vigorously and force-fed him luke-warm tea.

Shake, shake. "Get this inside you . . . "

Moan, moan. "I . . . understand . . . I understand." And so on throughout the night.

Dawn crept under the blanket of cloud slipping away to the west. Our col emerged from the greyness. Half a mile away, we could see the short snow slope leading to the lowest point on the ridge; on the far side, we knew, there was the 600-foot icewall. Cairns passed me yet another mug of that interminable tea.

He nodded at the sausage. "So, how is he?"

"Can't see him walking, what d'you think, Will?"

"How are we going to carry him?"

"Rope stretcher!"

"Rope stretcher?" Will and I repeated incredulously.

"I know how to make a rope stretcher!" Cairns announced with evident satisfaction.

"It goes like this . . . " Cairns uncoiled the rope. "You make a big loop here, then lay small loops across like this . . . " Soon Cairns had created the most incredibly complicated cat's cradle before our disbelieving eyes.

Okano, half-waking, began to sense the contraption was designed for him. He became restive, and looked worried as we approached him with ends of the ropes in our hands. "I understand . . . " he said with foreboding, as we trussed him up. It was becoming clear that Okano's one phrase conveyed something other than its literal meaning. And he was right to be concerned. In a little while he was tightly wrapped in the poleless tent, and tied up in ninety feet of rope.

We tried various combinations to carry Okano. One at each shoulder, and one at the feet; his head drooped. One each at the head, waist, and knees; Okano twisted excruciatingly. One at the head and one at the feet; we could not lift him. It was hopeless. We had no choice but to haul the painfully injured man across the glacier, over the avalanche tracks with their icy boulders. Where the slope changed angle, we would inadvertently roll him over. We man-hauled Okano barely half a mile, yet it took us four hours to reach the shallow col. Throughout the ordeal Okano grimaced bravely, but hardly suppressed his moans. All the time I fancied I could hear the broken ribs grinding.

The col had begun to seem like an unattainable horizon. Suddenly we breasted the edge, and gazed down the far side. Okano, though ashen with pain, was still with us. More than 600 feet below, miniaturised by the distance, a line of figures was traversing the Baintha Lukpar Glacier. The Japanese team. Only the ice face remained between us, the last barrier to Okano's survival. We waved, and sat Okano up to take in the scene, but it was all he could do to continue breathing.

It was on the third abseil that our rope stretcher began to unravel. Cairns and Will lowered Okano in a bundle from ice screws, while I was clipped to the ropes round Okano's legs. At the end of each pitch, I placed two more ice screws, and belayed Okano while the others abseiled down. We repeated the procedure twice without mishap. When the first loop uncoiled from the rope stretcher, Okano and I were no more than a hundred feet above the glacier. A hundred feet above safe and level ground. In a brief and unreasoning moment I supposed that we might both survive a hundred-foot fall, providing we missed the bergschrund. Another knot caught on the ice crust and began to work loose. A loop of rope snaked round Okano's face. I was horrified.

"Stop! . . . Stop! . . . Stop!" They could not hear me. I pulled myself up Okano, clambering over his broken body, clipped a krab into the dangerous loop and pulled it away from his face. Will and Cairns continued to lower us, more loops pulled apart. I fixed my jumar to the rope above Okano's head, and tied his harness directly to mine. Now we were dangling in space, slithering over the bergschrund. More loops fell away as the knots snagged on the edge of the schrund. We were lowered onto a shallow slope, and slid down to the flat glacier, and the waiting Japanese climbers. My legs had turned to jelly and, although I wanted to jump up and hug all three Japanese, the legs would not follow the mind. I was far too shaken to tell anybody how dangerous the last abseil had been. Okano rolled onto his side, and hoarsely intoned into the snow, "I . . . understand."

2

After the rescue, the Japanese moved their Base Camp down to join us, making a small village of tents which filled the hollow in the moraine. Omiya had sent a mail runner down to Skardu to call up a helicopter to fly Okano and himself out to hospital. Now Japanese and British climbers watched for it through binoculars. With a low rumbling, the helicopter wheeled round the heel of Mango Brakk, under Bakordas, which the British Women's Expedition had attempted in 1978, and wobbled up the Biafo Glacier. The rest of the Japanese team were going to trek out in six days. There was a shiver of expectation. The sun glinted off the helicopter as it followed the centre of the ice river until the pilot saw our landing zone, marked out with crossed Karrimats and stones. Banking steeply he slid down into our ablation valley.

I have wondered since that day exactly how much a military helicopter weighs. The machine keeps itself up by displacing its own weight of air, which it hurls downwards. It is a simple law of physics. Why this should keep several tons of metal suspended, I have never quite fully understood, but it does. The mistake we made was to overlook this law of physics. We had marked out a landing zone next to our tents. I began to feel uneasy as I watched the giant metal insect wobble over the moraine, blowing a mushroom of dust. My unease grew with the roaring. The helicopter floated over our tents like a steam roller. The poles snapped and the tents squashed as if some invisible monster had just trodden on them. The contents puffed out into the hurricane that marked the path of the machine. Karrimats, paperbacks and passports danced over the moraines and onto the glacier.

Three days later Cairns and our liaison officer were still picking bits of documents from the Biafo Glacier, while Will and I struggled up the Uzum Brakk Glacier. The sun burned my neck relentlessly. Will had become a distant speck crawling over the folds of the glacier. We were keeping to the middle to avoid the lateral crevasses, and following a shallow stream on the crunchy surface of the ice. This was, for Will and me, the third attempt to reach our prospective Advance Base. On the first occasion, it had taken us three days to reach the Thousand Foot Icefall which we failed to climb. Our second attempt with Cairns was interrupted by the rescue episode. This time we set out early, it was still night really, after a breakfast of eggs and parathas (fried chapatis). Staggering under twenty-kilo loads, we made our last farewells to the Japanese.

Cairns, who had not acclimatised as well as he wanted to, was not coming with us. Will and I left Base suffering slightly from diarrhoea. Mohamed Ali's food was good, but his washing up methods left much to be desired.

Glaciers are really the strangest environment. The Karakoram glaciers flow from the permanent winter of altitude down into the desert, where they melt in the sun and the sand. The snout of the Biafo lies buried under acres of moraine and hundred-foot waves of scree, rolling imperceptibly to the terminus. To say the Biafo is five miles wide and thirty-five long is rather missing the point of the terrain. With porters it takes four days to cover those thirty-five miles, and half a day to cross the ice. For most of its length the glacier visibly ablates under the tropical sun. Glacier tables, ice pinnacles, and foaming surface rivers are the landmarks on this desert of sun-baked ice. This is a zone of meltwater and evaporation. Crevasses here are safe because they are visible. In the

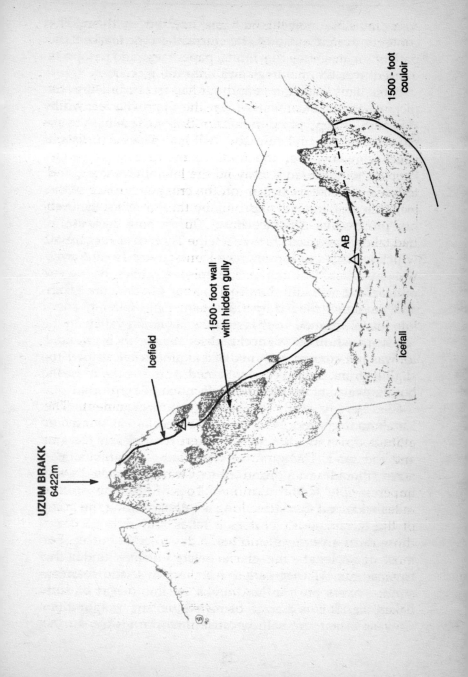

UZUM BRAKK
6422m

Icefield

1500 - foot wall
with hidden gully

AB

Icefall

1500 - foot
couloir

Ablation Zone objective dangers are few, but the toil is great under the sun. Will and I toiled on the Uzum Brakk Glacier.

At the head of our glacier, elegant and steep, Uzum Brakk dominated the horizon. Our mountain, first described to us as Conway's Ogre, was probably named by Martin Conway, who led the first major expedition to the Karakoram. In 1892 he surveyed and mapped vast areas connecting the Hunza valley to the Braldu and Baltoro system. One of his camps in July of that year was our Base. Just to the east, and 2830 feet higher than Conway's Ogre was the true Ogre (Baintha Brakk to the local people) invisible from Conway's Camp. Both these mountains feed the Uzum Brakk Glacier. Further east again the complex of peaks forming the Latok Group fed the west-flowing Baintha Lukpar Glacier. Two miles below the confluence with the Baintha Lukpar Glacier, the Uzum Brakk Glacier flowed into the giant Biafo Glacier, and it was at this branch, in the last green ablation valley on the Biafo, that Conway's surveyors had made their camp.

We had crossed the medial moraines that striped the Uzum Brakk, lines of heaped rubble, red rocks from the Latok peaks, black slate from an unnamed group of pinnacles near Baintha. The beating sun had made us strip down to the waist. Labouring under rucksacks the size of beer barrels, we climbed the treadmill of each moraine ridge. From the heights we could note a landmark, perhaps a boulder on a distant ridge, and as we picked a way through the troughs and valleys of shifting stones, climbed round boulders and slid down screes, our landmark, at first no bigger than a fist, would grow till it was the size of a small office block.

At one point it was easier to follow the dry pitted bed of a vanished surface stream. For an hour or so the miniature valley of rock-pimpled ice wound in slow curves towards Uzum Brakk. Rounding a bend, we walked straight into a wall of noise. A mighty foaming torrent was surging down our little valley. Yet, just feet from where we stood, it stopped. But ours was no parting of the Red Sea. We had not smitten the waters with our ice axe. There was a hole in the ice. The torrent roared into the chasm like an endless Pullman express.

There was a rock table not far from the swallow hole, where Will pulled out a stuff sack with our lunch. Carefully he separated the chapatis from the slightly crushed boiled eggs. Mohamed Ali had buttered the chapatis with ghee, and spread them with jam. We thought of him appreciatively as we watched the torrent leap into the hard glacier ice. The eggs were the last of our little store from Askoli and they had gone off. We threw them into the torrent and shouldered the enormous rucksacks again. The torrent snaked across the glacier, and after a while, as Will and I were beginning to grow accustomed to the noise, it began, just as suddenly as it had ended, in a fountain, there in the middle of the Uzum Brakk Glacier, for no apparent reason, a five-foot-wide frothing, eternal champagne pop.

I began to feel that I might be dreaming. Although we had been travelling for hours, clambering and falling over the rock-studded ice, there was still no change in perspective. The wind soughed through the granite pinnacles of Baintha and Uzum. For me it was new and frightening, to hear a wind a mile above us from the floor of this burning oven of a glacier. Were the spires cutting the wind into howling banshees? Was that a fatal wind to be caught in? Will had marched off into the distance and was now a speck on the next ridge. Alone with my thoughts I began to feel ill. The sun burnt my neck. The terraced masses of Baintha Brakk and the Aiguilles of Uzum towered over the glacier, where I crawled with the infinitesimal slowness of a mite on the folded hide of an elephant. I was insignificant, minuscule, on this unreal glacier. Distance, balance, place . . . all meant nothing. Wobbling I leant over, sank to my knees. My stomach kicked violently, retching. The sky darkened as I reached out, falling, falling.

After a while, it passed. I drank from a surface stream. Much revived, I saw that Will was barely visible on the folded horizon, yet I found this no longer depressing. I felt well! My sickness must have simply been due to Mohamed Ali's packed lunch and, if so, I would soon catch up William when he succumbed. I wondered as I marched purposefully up the glacier if all that mystical at oneness with the glacier and the mountain was merely the result of a bad paratha?

I caught up with Will in the late afternoon, as we approached the Dump, where we had cached our gear below our earlier high point on the Thousand-Foot Icefall. We could see that the Dump was inhabited. A pair of enormous black birds perched on our bivouac sacks as vultures do over a corpse. It was a sacrificial and ancient scene. Will, showing his classical education, began to tell me about the Roman habit of augury.

"There were various ways of forecasting, you could cut up a goat and examine its entrails. Or you could examine the flight of birds, ravens for example . . . "

The birds on our stores looked like ravens. In the distance across the shining glacier, they could have been black-cloaked priests examining the entrails of the bivouac sacks.

"So if the ravens flew to your right, the dextrous side, that was a good sign."

"And the left?"

"That is sinister."

We stopped to look at the ravens. They stopped to look at us. When they finally decided we had approached near enough, they spread their great wings, and lazily rose into the air.

"Himalayan choughs," said William, as they passed between us and the mountains on our left.

When we reached the scene of the augury, our beautiful

new Gore-tex bivouac sacks had been pecked through all over, and where a food box was revealed, the holes had been enlarged. Bits of food and wrapping lay all around. The foam mattresses had been holed. Feathers from the duvet jackets blew in the wind. Our food stores were ransacked. Would we risk psittacosis if we tried to salvage the part-eaten stores, and develop parrot fever half-way up the climb?

We laid out the sorry contents of the two sacks. The hardware was, of course, unscathed. Crampons and ice axes were indigestible, even for these formidable creatures. The ropes were okay. As for the food, it seemed that the birds had discreet tastes. The sweets were largely undamaged. The chocolate had been holed but no more, tea, barely pecked. The packets of instant rice all gone. The freeze-dried stews with dumplings devoured. The truly delicious instant banana custard eaten.

"Hey, have you noticed?"

"What?"

"It's the freeze-dried instant packages, they've eaten."

"You mean . . . "

"Yes, it proves they can read," said Will.

"Well, I'll be a monkey!"

The birds had only pillaged the packets clearly marked on the outside with the name of the manufacturer, Raven Products Ltd.

It began to rain. We set up the tent. Cooking under the fly sheet of the porch soon produced a warm fog, and later, a rain of condensation. We would not try to climb the Thousand-Foot Icefall in the morning. The last time dawn had found us near the top of the Icefall, surrounded by the most delicate and potentially devastating scenery, huge tottering towers in pastel shades, crumpled rose-coloured bridges, sea-blue chasms. We had raced dawn to the tent before the sun brought the entire glorious edifice down around us. The problem was in reaching the base of our mountain. The North Ridge was our proposed line.

This ridge marked the right edge of the East Face. Between the East Face and Baintha Brakk was a glacier basin, the Upper Uzum Brakk Glacier, at an altitude of about 16,500 feet. It was this glacier that spilled from the basin to form the Icefall. The Icefall was contained by granite pillars, impassable on the south side, but on the north side, our right, a thin couloir split the granite needles.

In the morning we weighed down the snowflaps on the tent with raven-proof rocks and, labouring under heavy rucksacks, threaded a line between the crevasses towards the couloir. It was a late start, and by sunrise we were still in the couloir. The dawn had been grey, a ceiling of cloud spread to the horizon. It was reasonable to hope that the sun might stay away. But it caught us in mid-couloir. The shadows retreated as we climbed. Man-eating blocks slid from their perches in the sun-softened ice as we passed them, but nothing was falling from above, so we pressed on. After six hours of pushing our loads up the collapsing couloir, a Sisyphean hell, we found a small rocky ledge twenty feet below the crest. We were exhausted. It took Will an hour to summon up the energy to flounder up those last few feet, I sat and watched. I saw him tentatively peep over the top of the col.

"Shi-i-yit!"

He meant that he could now see Uzum, and that he was impressed.

I joined Will after a decent interval. The entire basin lay before us, the Upper Uzum was as white and smooth as table linen. Immediately to our left was the rock spire guarding one side of our couloir. Beyond it the Icefall plunging a thousand feet to the glacier. On the far side, about half a mile away, a long and spectacularly aiguilled ridge abutted the smooth granite walls of Uzum's East Face guarding the Summit Icefields. From the right side of the East Face, the North Ridge appeared to run down to a series of high cols and aiguilles, before dancing fretfully up to Baintha Brakk. Opposite Uzum, the walls of Baintha, huge cliffs, 2000 feet high, layered with séracs, closed the ring. The only way down from the basin was over the Icefall.

Immediately below us a steep snow slope, of about 300 feet, gave access to the basin. It was barely midday. Avalanches were being triggered off by the sun almost everywhere. We decided to wait out the day on the col, leave our loads there, and carry up the rest of our equipment the next day. This waiting is of course the correct mountaineering decision. You are supposed to wait till nightfall, allowing time for the snow to refreeze. We did not have the patience, I am not sure I know anyone who has. As soon as the sun went off our slope at about 5.00 pm, we flung ourselves down it, sinking up to the knees, starting several sliding avalanches, and reached our tent within the hour.

We were back at the col above the Icefall by 6.00 am the next day. There was almost a hundred kilos of gear and food to lower down the 300-foot slope to the glacier. Will and I filled our chough-pecked bivouac bags and, tying our ropes together, lowered them to flat ground. We abseiled down after our loads, to be greeted by the walls of Baintha. There was a sharp crack, then thunder. As we watched, a large sérac slid from the top of the cliffs. A thousand tons of ice slipped out into space, floating weightlessly for the briefest of eternities, before exploding on the glacier floor. The ice dust blotted out the sun, and carried in the folds of a swirling wind, gently snowed on us.

It seemed like a good idea to tow half our load in the bivouac bags, rather than make two carries across the basin. The going was heavy, and when the sun broke out from the peaks around us, we fell victim to a terrible attack of Glacier Lassitude. By 10.00 am we had merely reached the middle of the basin. We could stagger no further. It now seemed like a good idea to pitch the tent, and call it Advance Base Camp. This was the third day in a row that we had been caught by the sun. We lay under the cover of the fly sheet, but found that though the light from the sun was blocked out by the tent fabric, the fabric was quite transparent to heat radiation which sapped all energy. It was an effort just to breathe. We spent the afternoon devising ways of blocking out the heat, and making desultory brews. Advance Base Lassitude had begun to set in. But with the sunset we recovered sufficiently to plod up the glacier basin to look at our proposed route. We were in for a shock.

The North Ridge did not exist! We had been completely deceived by the photographs. There were in fact three quite separate sections of ridge, divided by two bowl-shaped faces, and a large east-facing buttress. The bowl-shaped faces were unappealing, we did not have enough equipment to cross such a large wall of granite. Nor did we have sufficient bravery. We turned to go. The sun was setting in a boiling red sky. Our tracks led down to the centre of the glacier, where the tent glowed in the last rays of sunlight, at 17,000 feet, on an untrodden glacier in an unrescuable position. Surely this was the true meaning of splendid isolation. Will was enjoying this. He had a certain look in his eye that I had noticed before . . . perhaps the last of the Himalayan explorers?

When we reached the tent, I tried to get the petrol stove going while William performed his medical experiments. We had been given a grant of £400 for his work. The idea was to measure the strength with which we could expel our breath, and how this varied with altitude. It was not a measure of lung volume, but how hard we could blow. The apparatus was basic, two close-fitting cardboard tubes, one inside the other. The inside tube had a scale marked in litres/minute, which always seemed unrewarding for the amount of effort spent. William's job was to make us blow three times into the machine and record the results which he stored, together with the pencil, inside the tube. All very neat.

I was rather excited by the results. In Mrs Davies' Hotel in Rawalpindi, Cairns and William blew a magnificent eighty litres per minute, while I managed to wheeze a miserable fifty on the scale. By the time we reached Base I was catching up, I could manage sixty, while the others were down to seventy. Here at Advance Base, William and I were very nearly the same. Will told me sniffily that while the result might be very encouraging for asthmatics like me, the statistical sample was too small and therefore insignificant. But as I struggled with the stove, I knew I was going to be able to keep up with the bugger when we crossed that bergschrund.

It was taking me an age to get the petrol stove alight. Our strategy had been to take butane gas for the climbing and a light-weight petrol stove for use on the glaciers, manufactured by a Seattle-based firm producing a few highly specialised items. Another of these was a helmet the size, shape and colour of a Belisha beacon. I bought one when I started mountaineering, because the literature said that up to now all helmets had been designed to stop small stones or falling ice. This enormous helmet had been tested on dummies to prevent injury during a fall. Unfortunately the helmet was so large and heavy it was only suitable for dummies. I left mine stuck in a narrow chimney in the Alps, where as far as I know it still rests today, no doubt draped with abseil slings, because it bars all further progress on that line. I don't think one ever learns from mistakes.

"Blast, that's the third pricker I've broken today. There must be something wrong with the petrol."

"Why don't you admit it?" said Will, hungry but still gloating. "Your stove is bloody useless!"

It was true, the stove would only function with the greatest of difficulty. At Base Camp it was fine, but up here, the extra few thousand feet had done for it.

The next morning, 3rd August, the altimeter began to

rise. Counting the food store, we had two days' food for consumption at Advance Base, five days' climbing food, and soup cubes, coffee and sugary drinks for a further three days. If the weather was going to deteriorate, we would have to descend to Base, or risk climbing without a store of food at Advance Base to rely on.

We set off in the afternoon up and over the col, slip-sliding down the couloir, jumping the crevasses, striding out down the hard surface ice, back down the acres of moraine. Over and round the hundred-foot waves of scree, rolling imperceptibly downhill, running and leaping. We reached Base in six hours.

Mohamed Ali made suji (semolina) and cakes for us. He was pleased to see the expedition doctor as he had not slept for days. He had stomach aches, and his back hurt. On the 4th he cooked rice and sag (spinach) for supper. The sag had been left by an unknown porter. We toasted his health, and slept the sleep of the deserving.

After breakfast, our liaison officer, Farhut, said that he was going to wash in 'a nice warm pool' he had found nearby. As I had not washed since the hot springs of Chapko, almost a month earlier I joined him, relishing the valley smells of chives and wild garlic. But his pool was an icy muddy puddle in which I could only bring myself to dip my feet. While Farhut splashed himself all over with the repulsive liquid, I walked back to Base, looking for wild rhubarb to stew with sugar. Lunch was a chicken sent by the grateful Japanese, followed by rhubarb and Raven Products' Banana Custard . . . yum. The only trouble was the portions. Everyone seemed to be getting more than me! There was one of those scenes; after all, I reasoned, Will and I will be needing the food more than the others.

Farhut looked up sharply. "It is very bad manner to complain like this." He was very upset. I was angry, how could this slob be telling me about manners? We had risked our lives to rescue the Japanese climbers, not he.

The Japanese had sent three chickens to us in gratitude, yet, while Will and I were trying to fulfil the aims of the expedition, Cairns and Farhut had eaten two of them. At least, I thought, they might have offered us the last chicken before returning to the mountain. I seethed visibly.

William, English to the core, was deeply embarrassed. He started a conversation about the difficulty of making chapatis. Cairns laid out the pieces on the magnetic chess set, nodding as Will explained how he could never get his chapatis round. I walked out of the camp into the wild grass and herbs. A little later, Will and I packed as much food into our sacks as we could carry, and set out again for Advance Base. Dusk overtook us after we had passed the rolling moraines. We laid out the Karrimats and sleeping bags on the ice. The black sky was sprinkled with stars and dusted with galaxies. The following morning we reached Advance Base before the sun.

3

The north side of Uzum was not for us. We now knew there was no ridge, and the only line we could trace involved traversing the centre of a large slabby wall. But we had no spare rope for fixing this section, and so the traverse would be irreversible in a storm.

We examined the traverse. "Well?" asked Will.

"Looks hard. Hinterstoisser territory."

"Could we leave one of our ropes behind?"

"I wouldn't like to. We might need both ropes for abseiling, and also, we have no real idea how long the traverse is, one rope might not be enough."

An irreversible traverse, like the one that defeated Hinterstoisser and his party on the Eiger in 1936, was an epic to read about, not re-enact. But there was an alternative line. At first the magnificent East Face looked unbreachable. But after a great deal of arguing about it, we began to see a peculiar diagonal line splitting the Great Wall. Here was a possible line to the summit icefields. The diagonal line did seem to peter out rather, and perhaps we might be left with some hard face climbing but, surely, we reasoned, something would turn up. Closer inspection showed our diagonal line to be a gully hidden by a whale-back fin of granite. It was a natural avalanche trap. Each morning, at 10.30, the sun would spread out onto the East Face. Slabs of snow and ice relinquished their struggle against gravity and poured down the diagonal gully like giant concrete. This was the only thing wrong with our proposed route.

"At night, it could be very safe," I offered.

"But can we climb it all at night? What if we get caught by the day?" William was concerned.

"Perhaps, we can sort of cling to the sides?"

"Don't be an idiot, Saunders."

I don't think Will appreciated the vision, the two of us clinging, like rats to the side of a surging drain.

"Well, it is probably over 3000 feet. If we start after supper, we should be near the top of the gully by dawn. It will need soloing as much as possible, of course. Also, if you look, about two-thirds of the way up. See?" There was a niche on the right side of the gully, under an overhanging wall. It looked as if there should be a decent shelter from rockfall, as well as the main gully avalanches.

"Hmmph . . . " Will was not prepared to be convinced, but he did not disagree.

That evening we dined on Spicy Beef and Complete Potato mix. It was meant to be a treat. We packed our sacks, we were still expecting Cairns to turn up at any moment. Will wrote a message for him and hung it prominently in the tent. "We leave at 10.00 pm on 6.8.80, planning to climb all night. We plan the couloir route and hope to be up most of it by daybreak. My camera is in the orange, green and white bag. Film is finished and re-wound, but still in camera. Filter (Y/6 for B/W on camera, clear for colour in bag). Food for you is in yellow stuff sack (dehydrated and oatcakes) and Karrimor sack (brews, sweets and chocolates etc): other stuff sack is hill food. Love and kisses. Will."

With the paprika still rising in our throats, we crossed the bergschrund at 11.00 pm. We had stopped below it to tie on the ropes and eat half a chocolate bar, cocooned under our anorak hoods. Other than the occasional rush of spindrift whispering on the nylon and our noisy breathing, there was silence. And the silence was black. Stars pricked the sky; a faint, subliminal phosphorescence hovered above, indicating the icefields we knew were there. We were both nervous. Months of effort had been dedicated to this moment. We had travelled 4000 miles by machine, and fourteen days on foot, to reach this place. We had completed the syllabus, now we were walking into the exam.

By dawn we found ourselves a thousand feet above the glacier, taking turns to lead out pitches on the ice. It was straightforward ice climbing, fifty degrees from the horizontal. Although the night sky had been clear, the dawn brought with it a blanket of thin grey cloud. Opposite us, Baintha Brakk, the Ogre, had developed a classic storm cap. At 10.00 am, after eleven hours of continuous climbing, we reached our Niche. We were exhausted. The rucksacks must have weighed twenty kilos. The ledge at the Niche was not as comfortable as we had hoped, as it sloped steeply. Will hammered in a peg above our heads, I lassoed some spikes which I assured Will were not loose. We settled down to make a brew and watch the weather. The telltale cap on Baintha grew larger, the grey blanket drew closer and began to develop a banded pattern, like the back of a mackerel.

"What do you think?" asked Will.

"Mackerel sky. Storm caps. If this was the Alps, I'd go down immediately. It would probably mean a ten-day storm."

"Do you think the weather patterns are the same here?"

"I don't know, but I don't think we should hang about to find out."

It was almost midday, but the cloud cover protected the East Face from the sun. While there was cloud cover, there would be no avalanches ... we hoped. So we decided to abseil off immediately. We hung our spare rock pegs, gas cylinders and food inside a large stuff sack, belayed to the ledge. In order to protect our limited quantity of ice screws, we attached lengths of pink ribbon to each abseil point on the way down, in order to be able to find them quickly when we returned after the storm. We had bought the ribbon in Rawalpindi, and were pleased with our foresight.

I left the ledge first and as I lowered myself, I noticed a few loose flat stones lying in the corner. Slow deliberate care with rope techniques was the habit I had learned from the Alps. I had had my share of fiasco, dropped pegs, karabiners, descenders, even ice axes; but I had learned from these mistakes. The possibility of cutting the abseil ropes while still a thousand feet up a big face, held only terror for me so I pushed the rocks out of the way of the tight ropes. It's not the climbing, it's the abseiling off that kills.

When it came to Will's turn to abseil, he must have knocked those rocks down. I had fixed the first ice screw, clipped myself into it, and was fixing the second, when I heard Will's shout.

"BELOW! . . . "

I looked up at the wrong instant. Rocks were whirring in the air. Quite suddenly there was blood spattered on the ice in front of me. Lots of it. At first I couldn't work out what had happened. Blood everywhere, my clothes, gloves, on the ice. There was a bloody tooth stuck in the ice. I had been hit in the face.

"My God, I've loft my teef . . . " I seemed to be spraying more blood over my gloves. I lost consciousness for a few minutes. (Simply can't stand the sight of my own blood.)

When Will arrived at the belay, he was having difficulty with his left crampon and was hardly able to look after himself, while I suffered recurring fainting fits. It took us a very long time to abseil down the thousand feet of ice. Eventually Will's crampon refused to go back on his boot. I lowered him the last 300 feet, threw the ropes down and soloed after him, trailing blood, spit and self-pity. The sky was darkening when we reached the glacier, the ropes had frozen like wire hawser. We forced them into bends, and stuffed them over the rucksacks, tying the lids down as tight as possible. The tent, so small and isolated from the Niche, welcomed us home as we unzipped the fly sheet. Will's note to Cairns was untouched. It was 1.00 pm on 7th August, just thirty-six hours since we had left the tent.

That night I felt awful, in more misery than pain. In fact I had lost only one tooth, the front right upper, and I was able to take food, sipping birdwise with my head turned sideways, as Will fixed up brews of Sweet and Sour Chicken. But now I was to be scarred, gap-toothed. The insult to vanity hurt far more than the injury. It snowed all night long, and Will and I spent much of it banging the walls of the tent to shed the compressing snow that threatened to collapse it. We were experiencing our first Karakoram storm.

We spent the next five days confined to the tent. Will consoled me. "At least your mouth will have a chance to heal without infection." During those days we talked and read. Every twelve hours or so we had to pull on our waterproofs to dig out the tent. Will finished Thomas Pynchon's *V* on 9th August, and, passing it to me, announced that he was now out of books. He made a chess set out of bits of silver paper and the cardboard from a packet of biscuits.

Till now, I hardly knew Will. We were not friends before the trip, we had only climbed once together. Our pre-Karakoram training consisted of a rain-soaked weekend on Ben Nevis during February, and a few lively discussions in assorted pubs. Yet now we were forced together, day after day, in a space no larger than that under a table. Will had read medicine at Oxford and Edinburgh, where he met Cairns. Cairns, squinting through his John Lennon glasses, with his slightly supercilious attitude to anything English, was the more remote of the two. Or so I thought.

At the beginning of the year, Cairns and Will were

working in Edinburgh, while I lived in a tiny terrace house in London's East End. They had sent down a removal van full of waxed cardboard boxes which completely filled my house and it took weeks of rewriting lists and muddled packing before the seventeen boxes were ready to be air freighted out to Rawalpindi. I was delegated to buy the air tickets, which I got from an extremely sleazy bucket shop in Soho. Naturally I got the dates confused, and the three of us turned up at Heathrow the day after our flight. It hadn't been a really good start to an expedition with near strangers.

Will's attitude to expedition medicine was interesting. After one particularly strenuous fit of packing and repacking, we retired to the Spread Eagle where he became expansive.

"Of course," he said, "if it can be cured on expedition it must be trivial. We certainly won't be needing a stethoscope."

Four weeks later we were in Skardu, trying to select our porters from a band of frightening ruffians. Will decided to listen to their chests. He put two fingers on their backs and asked them to breathe in deeply. There was no response, so he asked them again, slower and louder. Will eliminated the chronic asthmatics, and told eight of the men to meet us at Bongla Bridge. The men would walk the fifty miles to Bongla, while we travelled by overloaded jeep.

Our driver took a callow youth to mend the road where it had washed away. At one torrent, we all chose to wade the icy water rather than risk floating down to the Indus with the jeep. In spite of the river crossings, it was a dry, rock-strewn track and we were yellow with dust by the time the jeep pulled up under a lonely apricot tree in the middle of a desert, which the driver said was Bongla Bridge. Cairns, Will and I eased ourselves out of the jeep, and wandered about in a bemused state. After about ten minutes, our chosen porters and their friends materialised, I felt even more bemused. We needed six more porters, and once again Cairns and I were privileged to witness that wonderful performance in clear, slow, and very loud English.

"Now please, INHALE . . . DEEPLY."

We walked and lived in the aroma of the men for the next eight days. They smelled of juniper wood, which they used for cooking. Our porters were Baltis, and this was Baltistan. Some were Ismaili, but most of the men were Shia Muslims. They wrote in the cursive Urdu script, but their language, Balti, was an ancient dialect of Tibetan. My notebook steadily filled with Balti words as we walked in. Some of the words were astonishing. For instance, there were different names not only for yesterday, today and tomorrow, but also for the day after tomorrow, and the day after that. And the word meaning yes could also mean good, real and very. Perhaps most astonishing of all to me were the numerals, which were recognisably the same as the Japanese numbers. How could this be?

What may have been obvious to a trained linguist, was to me, on my first visit to the great ranges, exciting. I pondered the problem. Throughout the walk in to Base I pondered the problem. Increasingly fanciful explanations suggested themselves. I looked at our Balti porters and dreamed of lost tribes, and centuries of wandering nomads criss-crossing the steppes of Central Asia. For some reason I was slow to ask the Japanese, and when I did, Omiya explained the mystery to me in two short sentences. "Buddha!" he said, "Buddha is reason for numbers same. We have same culture, see?" He pronounced culture 'car-jur'. He also used Palis for Paris, and on one occasion actually referred to both "Rondon and Palis" in the same sentence, which gave me unaccountably childish delight.

Will found it hard to be immobilised during the storm when he finished the Pynchon. I continued to lose battles with the stove. We tapped the altimeter, kept thumping the tent walls and talked of feasts at home. On 12th August we packed our sacks for a last attempt to climb the route. Will wrote another message for Cairns on the back of an oatcakes packet, which he jammed prominently in the zip. At midnight we crossed the bergschrund for the second time. Our rucksacks were full, the beam of the head torch narrow, the ice firm and cold. As we drove the axes into the white wall, the ice squeaked. Only the best ice does this, it has to be cold and dry and of the consistency of Styrofoam. We climbed solo, each trailing a rope. By dawn we reached our previous high point. Above us the ice ramp disappeared, squeezed between two walls of granite. A thin ribbon of ice, like a frozen brook, followed the steep corner for about 500 feet. We could see no more of the route. We stopped at the rock-strewn Niche where Will fixed a belay and I made a brew, carefully shielding the gas stove with my legs. I did not want to drop any part of the stove or pan. The sky was clear, and the sun began to warm the East Face. Soon our route would be like a bowling alley. We would have our brew of instant chocolate, and wait for dusk. This was our plan. But friendly clouds invaded the sky and, seizing our chance, we started on the steep ribbon of ice. Will led the first pitch, the twin ropes followed, zigzagging between the ice screws. He was sending down showers of ice.

It was a little bit frightening. The ice here was brittle, no longer the reassuring Styrofoam squeak. The characteristic sound of brittle ice is the tinkle. Brittle ice is like glass, it shatters under the ice axe, and you have to kick the crampon again and again before you feel confident enough to step up. The ice radiates deep cracks where it has been hit, and sometimes breaks away in pieces the size and shape of dinner-plates. Dinner-plating always happens without warning. Will was about twenty feet above his last ice screw, and had not moved for ages.

"How's it going?" I shouted.

"It's dinner-plating!"

"Well, then, get a runner in!"

"I am trying to, but the ice keeps plating off."

After a while Will found that he could edge sideways towards a crack in the granite walls that contained the ice ribbon. He placed two Clog Stubby Channel pegs in the crack, and shouted down that he now had a belay. It had been a good lead. We climbed three more pitches of the ribbon. The climbing was steep work, and tiring on the arms but not nearly as tiring on them as it was on the brain.

The top of the ribbon merged into an area of snow-covered rocks, indeterminate buttresses and vague gullies, most of which led up into dead-endings, closed by more small overhanging outcrops. At last we were free of the ghastly brittle ice, and although the snow here was powdery and loose, the angle had eased off to fifty degrees. After an hour hacking out a small ledge in an arête of snow, we were able to hang up the bivouac tent.

This was our first night in it. We were proud of the design which was extremely simple. The bivouac tent was simply the inner tent from the one we used at Advance Base. The outer, or fly, containing the poles, was left on the glacier. The inner weighed a few ounces, and we had sewn small nylon slings through the ridge to provide belay points so that we would remain tied in at all times. In time you get used to your umbilical cord. You just have to be careful not to melt it while cooking, and you can never quite close the sleeping bag properly, but when you get back to Base, you cannot help feeling something is missing as you roll over unimpeded.

Looking out of the entrance to the tent we watched the fading alpenglow on Baintha Brakk. We could see the entire Scott-Bonington route. Our gloved hands traced their line of dire descent. The story of Doug Scott's broken legs and Chris Bonington's broken ribs, so close below the 23,900-foot summit they had just achieved, haunted our waking dreams, along with the Japanese parallel in which we had so recently been involved.

The ramp had taken us in to the heart of the East Face of Uzum Brakk. Below us was a 1500-foot vertical wall. Somewhere above was an icefield leading to the crest of the mountain. It was a nice situation, precarious and pregnant with anticipation. Happily and anxiously I started the evening routine of brews. Will struggled out of his overclothes and into his sleeping bag. Soon it would be my turn to struggle into the sleeping bag, while Will made the hot chocolate. It had been a long day.

It took two hours to get going in the morning. We had set the alarm for 5.00 am. The air was bitter, the soft fluffy snow chilled our toes and fingers. We each took a Ronicol tablet to enhance the peripheral circulation. The next pitch was mine. I traversed a few feet to reach the bottom of a gully filled with rotten ice. This area was the key to the climb. If only we could find a way to connect the Ramp with the Icefield, I felt sure we could climb the mountain. The ice in the gully provided no support, and I tried to clamber onto a shallow buttress, but the rock was blank except for a thin crack. I wedged an axe in the crack, and panting heavily pulled my weight onto the axe. My crampons were scratching about unnervingly. I punched the hammer into the crack and tried to pull myself up that too, gasping for air.

"Arghh . . . gasp . . . It's no good, Will, I'm coming off. Watch the rope . . . " I managed to reverse the move without losing my balance. "Perhaps we can go sideways a bit."

"Good, I was about to untie," William replied encouragingly.

Just for that I cut an enormous resting ledge, and showered him with the ice. The next three pitches took us across the Traverse, a narrow band of easy-angled snow resting above the enormous East Wall. The loose snow slid off the ledges, drifting across the 1500-foot wall below us. Our traverse led to the Great Icefield. At 3.00 pm we had reached a small buttress on its edge where we cut a ledge from the ice and set up our bivouac tent.

The next morning was very cold. As soon as we pulled our boots on, our feet seemed to turn to blocks of ice. We took a Ronicol each with our tea, packed the tent by torchlight, and set off onto the cold, dark ice face. It was a concave face, which gradually steepened as the tangible blackness was displaced by grey horizons. We took turns to lead, and stopped counting the pitches, our minds numb with the cold and effort of pushing our rucksacks up the ice face. When dawn came, it broke like an egg, all over the summit and down the sides. By the time we reached the upper edge of the Great Icefield, we were both blinking in the gelid glare. We stopped to share a Mars bar. Above us a steep-looking pitch led straight up towards the fretsaw summit ridge. The pitch was even steeper than it looked, flakes of rock stuck out of the ice, and we hooked our ice axes over these, kicking out with the crampons and shattering the brittle ice. The effort burned our muscles, flames of agony consumed the arms and legs. We were drawn and ashen as we pulled ourselves onto the summit ridge. And here was the cruellest blow, the snow was like a hay rick. Straw snow, it had no load-bearing strength, yet the ridge sported several large cornices and double mushrooms. We were so near the summit, we were on the summit ridge, yet there was the highest point, just fifty feet higher than us, just 400 yards away.

"What do you think?"

"It's too dangerous and, look, the weather is breaking up."

It was true, dark clouds menaced the western horizon. Already Snow Lake and the Hispar Glacier lay under the evil shadow.

"Let's give it an hour and see?"

"Okay."

The hour was wasted wallowing across the unstable double cornices. We realised it was time to turn back, without regret. A few precarious abseils from the teetering cornices brought us down to the icefield by dusk. The wind was beginning to pick up. We down-climbed the ice to save our ice screws and, reaching our bivouac ledge of the previous night, happily set about the routine. To supplement the three evening drinks, we opened a celebratory tin of sardines to smear on the four oatcakes.

"Will?"

"Mmm?" picking sardine droppings from his beard.

"If the weather holds, we might just make it down to the glacier by tomorrow night, Base by the 17th. I could be in London in ten days with luck."

"Why worry?"

"My holiday leave ends today." Just think, I thought, I could be watching *Dr Who*, slipping down those sherbets in the Spread Eagle, topping up with a chicken vindaloo . . . but here I am.

Of course it did not work out like that. The next day the blizzard struck and we could not leave our ledge. The day after that, we realised we did not have enough food to sit out a storm, and tried to climb out of it. My glasses froze over, and no amount of wiping could remove the rime from the lenses. With frozen limbs we inched our way down the ice by feel. In the blizzard we nearly missed the line of the Traverse, and almost abseiled into the void of the East Wall. It took five hours to descend two and a half pitches. With exposure and exhaustion setting in, our fingers fumbled the simple operations required to set up the bivouac. We now had no food left. The following day we could only traverse three pitches. At this rate of progress, it would be another week before we could reach our tent.

I was getting concerned when, after three days of continuous blizzard, the dawn brought clear skies. The chalk-dusted peaks bore witness to the long storm as they leant together overlooking the silent glaciers. Hurried abseils brought us down to the tent, and two days after that Will and I staggered into Base, dwarfed by thirty-kilo loads. We had been away for sixteen days, and Cairns had feared the worst. He and Farhut, our liaison officer, had struck the tents and were about to abandon us, leaving a note and some cans. They were not to know, I suppose, that neither Will nor I possessed a can-opener.

PART TWO

Bojohaghur, 1984

Map 2

△ Peak heights in metres

4

I don't know if Uzum Brakk was a success. How do you measure success? By what criteria did we measure our expedition? The objectives were obvious enough: to climb the mountain; to have a good time, whatever that may mean; to return unharmed. In reverse order of importance, of course.

We did return relatively unharmed. So the most important objective was fulfilled. A good time? Well, Will has not been to the greater ranges since, and that was nine years ago. Neither has Cairns. On the other hand we met and enjoyed the company of the Japanese climbers. There was a sincere, if temporary, friendship. After the expedition was over, the Japanese expedition physician, Dr Noda, visited us in England. Omiya and Okano sent all of us a year's subscription to the *National Geographic Magazine*, and a copy of the Japanese volume, *Mountains of the World*, a superb coffee-table book with pictures of all the mountains we had ever heard of, and many more that we had not.

Did we get up our peak? Er, nearly, perhaps, by Alpine standards. We climbed the route, to emerge on the summit ridge. Calvin Torrans, the Irish climber, once said that he climbed only for the route and not to bag the summit. If the summit were just twenty feet beyond the logical top of the climb, he would descend without covering those twenty feet. "You're just a crag rat, a mountaineer would never say that," I had replied. But now I could see the advantages of being a crag rat.

But there was another factor, one we had not fully understood before setting out, and that is the effect an expedition has on you. I cannot speak for Cairns and Will, but I think they too found the trip a powerful experience. The expedition almost certainly changed my life. During those eight weeks I had lived with an intensity I had not known was possible. I had stepped through a window into a world quite separate from, and parallel with, the world I had inhabited till then. That window was not to open again for four years.

Pints of beer and idle conversation in the Globe always led to ludicrous proposals, some of which came to fruition; driving 1500 miles to north-west Scotland and back almost every weekend during a fine winter spell; flying to the Alps for the weekend to attempt a winter ascent of the Walker Spur; climbing the chalk cliffs at Dover, by means of axes and crampons. Projects at which any right-thinking sober person should look askance became reasonable and normal. So it was that in 1982, assorted members of the North London Mountaineering Club (a club whose main cause for existence was the pints and idle conversation of the Globe) vowed to attempt to climb Bojohaghur, a peak of 24,044 feet (7329 metres) in the Western Karakoram.

There were six of us slumped around the beer-flooded table. It was the same group of six who two years later set out for Pakistan. I had just returned from the Bernese Oberland with Phil Butler, Phil was lean and brown from the holiday. The other four had returned from Tauliraju, in Peru, a week earlier: Mike (Boydie) Morrison, a mechanical engineer from Croydon, John English, a dermatologist, working in St John's Hospital for Skin and Venereal Diseases, Chris Watts, then manager of Alpine Sports, and Mick Fowler, tax collector. Fowler and Watts had lost a great deal of weight. Through all the laughing banter it was clear that the climb of Tauliraju had been hard and unforgiving.

The object of attention was my copy of *Mountains of the World*, which I was trying to keep dry.

"And that," I said, pointing at a poor colour picture of a deep ravine and a mountain lost in clouds, "is the highest unclimbed peak in Pakistan."

The others peered at the gloomy photograph. "Ultar? Never heard of it."

"The only problem is that Ultar is reserved for Pakistani parties only. Still, its sister peak, Bojohaghur Duanasir is almost the same height, and that does not seem to be reserved, nor has it ever been attempted."

"Probably because no-one has worked out how to pronounce it yet." A murmuration of guffaws circulated the table. But we were ignorant, even as we drank our beer a Japanese university club were returning home, beaten by the mountain.

"How much is it going to cost?" asked Fowler, setting aside the tax in his mind.

"Well, that's the great thing," I said. "It's right by the road! I am ninety per cent sure this picture was taken from the Karakoram Highway. We'll have virtually no porter fees, and that was by far the major cost of our Uzum Brakk trip. I was in the RGS Library yesterday . . . "

"Just for a change, ha ha," said John.

I ignored the diversion, and continued. "I measured the distance on a map, from the road to the top of Bojohaghur, it's only five miles."

"That's less than the walk-in to Craig Meghaidh!"

"So why hasn't anyone else done it?"

"Could be because no one else has thought of it," I said. "Or it might possibly be the vertical interval."

"What do you mean?"

"Well, as far as I can make out from the maps, this village here, Baltit, is at about 7000 feet. The mountain is 24,044 feet. So even if we establish a base, say 5000 feet higher than Baltit, it still leaves a vertical interval of 12,000 feet." (In fact we had slightly underestimated the vertical interval which was the equivalent of two and a half Eigerwands.)

"Which is obviously not easy, or it would have been done by now," said Phil.

I closed the book, and put it in my rucksack as someone kicked the table. A wave of beer ran across the surface, and dribbled over the edge. It was time to order more pints. We were still in fantasy land. From the safety of the pub, we could climb any mountain. Yet somehow this one refused to go away. Perhaps it was because we couldn't get any decent pictures of the peak, or perhaps it was the prospect of running the most impecunious ever expedition to a new 7000-metre peak.

The Karakoram Highway, built across Pakistan with Chinese help, provides a ribbon of tarmac, like any English B road, all the way from Rawalpindi to Kashgar. It means you can travel to the Karakoram by public transport. The one way in which the road differs from an English road is the war of attrition with nature. The road was built across some of the least stable land in the world, not just cliff faces, but across avalanche outfalls and permanent scree slopes. And nature is not kind in the mountains, she always wants to take back what is hers. To keep the road open is a continual battle with the forces of entropy; the bridges want to revert to ravine, and are frequently torn away by surging torrents; the roads want to turn back into open hillside, and seem to invite landslides. As if in recognition of this war, each section of the road is maintained by a Company of the Pakistan Army Road Maintenance Corps.

"The 42nd Coy wishes you a safe journey!" The sign was teetering on the brink of an abyss. The battered Ford Transit coughed, rattled to a halt under an overhang of loose reddish rock, and the driver flung himself under the engine muttering dire threats against the impassive machine. We unfolded our shaken bodies and, still vibrating, walked like drunken men towards the sign. We had been travelling nearly twenty hours. One by one we sat on the low stone wall that marked the edge of the bend, and looked down. A thousand feet below the Hunza river snaked across the ravine bed, a dusty strip of desert dotted with thorn bushes. By the river a patch of colour and a long smudge of black soot attracted our attention.

"Hey, Mahmud, what is that?" Phil asked the driver's mate.

"Bus, sixty-four people killed . . . look there!" Mahmud pointed to a tear in the wall near where we sat. We understood that the bus had missed the bend at that point. None of us slept on the Transit again, and there was some desperate bargaining to be near the door.

As the Highway follows the Hunza valley across the Karakoram it is overwhelmed by arrays of famous massifs. Nanga Parbat, where in 1895 A. F. Mummery was last seen, and in 1934 Willo Welzenbach, perhaps the greatest ice climber of the time, died a true Munich hero's death; Rakaposhi, whose first ascent by the evergreen Mike Banks and Tom Patey is hilariously recorded on film; Kunyang Chish, Batura, Trivor and many others. The road wound round the cliffs and landslips flinging us from one side of the Transit to the other, as we tried to ascribe names and histories to the mountains we passed under. It was Tilman who once said, "The identification of distant peaks is a safe and harmless pastime, provided it is not taken too seriously."

The Hunza valley springs from the edge of the Wakhan Corridor, a single Afghani valley system which separates Pakistan from the Soviet Union. The language of the inhabitants of the Upper Hunza indicates their ancestral migrations; they speak Wakhi, a dialect of Persian. Lower down the river system is the fertile oasis of Hunza and Nagar, ancient and permanently warring mirdoms, facing each other across the roaring Hunza. Here the language is the extremely complicated Burushaski. D. L. Lorimer, political agent in Gilgit, and later in Chitral, wrote in 1939, that Burushaski is unrelated to any known language. There are perhaps 10,000 speakers of Burushaski, which does not appear to have a written form. Below Hunza and Nagar the valley closes up, providing splendid natural defences. The river is disgorged at Gilgit, where it joins the Indus, and here in the lower reaches of the Hunza river they speak Shina, an Aryan language related to the main language groups of the Indian sub-continent.

In 1984 there were just six so-called hotels in Baltit. After a total of twenty-four hours of torture by baking and shaking, the Transit deposited us at the New Park Hotel, whose owner must have been the cousin of Mahmud, judging by the degree of choice we were given. The expedition had grown in size since leaving the Globe. We had acquired three-quarters of a ton of equipment, Mick's father, George Fowler, a trekking friend of Mick's, Steve Prendergast, a liaison officer, Captain Liaquat Hiat, and a leader, me. Though the team's interpretation of this role was more of general servant than generalissimo.

Kalb Ali, the proprietor of the New Park Hotel, beamed, he was all smiles. "Supper," he said. He was a man of few words. The expedition was billeted in adjoining rooms, surrounded and overwhelmed by their baggage. The members emerged from dark recesses of the inn like locusts to the feast. The table was spread with an assortment of curries, chips, omelettes, salads of cucumber and bowls of rice. Kalb Ali smiled and hovered, we tasted the food and showered praises. It was good. The first really good food for days since and, though we were not to know it, for days to come. We leant back in the chairs, returning Kalb Ali's smiles. The few remains were cleared away and Kalb Ali and his son brought bowls of ripe apricots and tea. "Thank you, that was really lovely." Kalb Ali beamed with appreciation.

After supper he asked us if we needed porters, we said

yes, and about ten minutes later a crowd of would-be porters were milling around our equipment. There was no point in John conducting a medical. The trek would take no more than eight hours the men assured us, so we got down to pay bargaining immediately. It was then that Liaquat proved his worth. When they demanded an exorbitantly high rate for the walk, he lined them up, stood them to attention, and harangued them in Urdu. He treated them like Sepoys on the verge of desertion. If he had had a pistol, I have no doubt that he would have started waving it about. After twenty minutes the men capitulated, and eventually everyone agreed to meet at dawn the next day.

It now remained for us to select a cook, and once again, we seemed to have no choice. I was beginning to suspect we weren't the only people running the expedition. The only man to present himself for this job was a wall-eyed arthritic called Hadayat Shah. He had not been a cook before, but said that he taught English in the school.

"Seems about as good a qualification for cooking as any other," said John.

"Hadayat Shah's a bit of a mouthful," Boydie said, "we'll call you Dai. Okay?"

Hadayat fixed him with his bad eye, and said, "I will come whenever you call me."

"No, no, I mean we'll *call* you Dai, okay?"

"Yes, I will come . . . "

"I wonder," John mumbled to himself, "if his cooking is better than his English."

Dai felt that an expedition cook deserved a somewhat higher rate of pay than we had anticipated. Using Liaquat to translate, we struck a bargain. We would pay Dai all he asked, but twice a week he would descend to Baltit for fresh supplies of vegetables, eggs, and chickens.

The topography of the Bojohaghur Group is complicated by the fact that it straddles the Karakoram Highway. It is almost impossible to stand back for a good view.

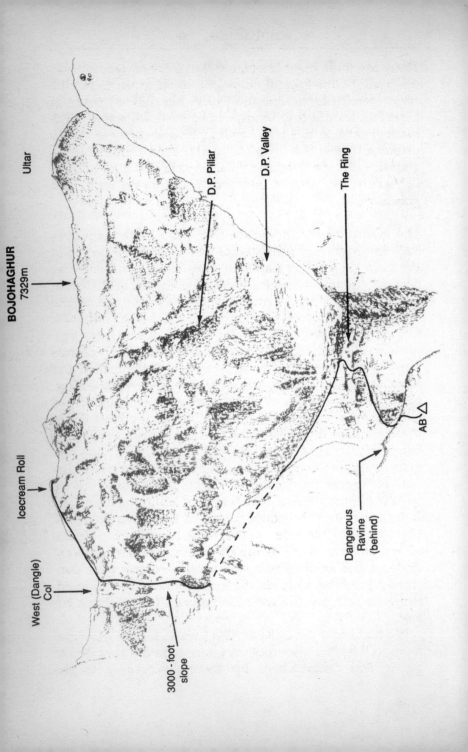

BOJOHAGHUR
7329m

Ultar

D.P. Pillar

D.P. Valley

The Ring

Icecream Roll

West (Dangle) Col

3000 - foot slope

Dangerous Ravine (behind)

AB

There are three main facets, but the only one we saw was the huge South Face. Bojohaghur stood at the back of a cirque four miles across, the 24,238-feet (7388m) peaks of Ultar I and Ultar II to its right, and more unnamed 7000-metre peaks to the left. Leading to one of these was a prominent shoulder of rock, which soon caught Mick's attention. Death Potential Pillar he called it. DP Pillar, as it became, was about one and a half miles high, and gruesome.

The main bowl of the South Face must have been over 8000 feet high, and consisted of tiers of séracs, grouped at the back of the bowl and on both sides, all funnelling down to a narrow hanging glacier at the base of DP Pillar. The hanging glacier terminated at a unique feature, the Ring. The Ring was the source of the Lower Ultar (or Lower DP, according to Fowler) Glacier. It was quite simply a semi-circle of ice-polished cliffs, with a generous topping of séracs. Billowing avalanches often filled the bowl, swept across the hanging glacier, and over the Ring. Mick called the entire bowl DP Valley, and its glacier, DP Glacier. Somewhat to the left of DP Pillar the West Ridge of Bojohaghur dipped down to a col at around 19,500 feet, before rising once again to crest Hunza Peak, and the granite spire of Bublimiting, which terminated the ridge with an exclamation mark. A glacial basin below the col fed the Hunza Glacier, which in turn led to the Ring. The Ring articulated the convergence of the Hunza and DP Glaciers, the left side of the Ring bearing the Hunza séracs, and the right side the DP séracs. These séracs were under considerable pressure to move on, and were constantly grinding towards the edge, where they toppled, lemming fashion, towards the Lower Ultar, 650 feet below.

We had hired ten of Kalb Ali's friends for the trek from Baltit to Base; we were not very sure where we wanted to go, it was "somewhere up there", according to the photograph, but Hassan, apparently the men's leader, seemed to know where to take us. We followed the edge of a narrow canal of pearly mica-filled melt water. As we left Baltit, our canal was joined by another branch. Hassan pointed and said "Karimabad", and soon another, where Hassan said "Berishal". He explained that all the villages derived their water from these canals, and each branch fed a separate village. Apparently, though we had just been walking through Baltit, our hotel was in Karimabad. Berishal was yet another small village that looked to the outsider as if it was an indivisible part of Baltit. All over the Karakoram the mountain villages are fed by canals like these. In Hunza they are called Go-Tsil, Tsil is the Burushaski for water, and Go is from the English. The Burushaskis are fond of the word Go, and where Urdu-speaking porters rise with great shouts of "Jello, Jello . . . Ji!", the Hunza men cry "Going, going . . . " It took me a while to realise they meant it.

We followed the Baltit Go-Tsil across a steep moraine, through apricot orchards and eventually to the mouth of the Ultar Nullah, the enormous black canyon above Baltit. Incredibly, the ancient Hunzakuts had engineered several Go-Tsil high on the huge walls, thin vegetated lines, weeping greenery at the leaks. After the hot dry dust of Baltit, the canyon provided a welcome shade. At the top of the canyon lay the snout of the Lower Ultar Glacier, a sleeping dragon, ever threatening the villages below, and on the right bank, some goat pastures which were as far as the Hunza men would go. It had taken them just four hours to complete the walk, though I struggled in some hours after everyone else. This Base Camp was half a mile below the Ring and at a little under 10,000 feet, far too low, but it was flat, there was a spring to one side, and conveniently rocky lavatory slopes down-wind. To the west, green-brown hills rose to a fretful sharpness on the horizon, while to the east, the slopes ran down to a small stream guided by the lateral moraine. It was very pleasant, the mountain was attractively remote.

Phil immediately began to set up house. The kitchen was to be a low stone enclosure against a large boulder, with our tarpaulin draped over, the food must be stored here, and the fire-place must go there, a drainage channel needed to go round the wall like this – more boulders – and so the work went on. Phil enjoyed kitchen-building. The men had charged us for at least eight hours' work, and so some of them stayed for an hour or so to help us collect boulders for the kitchen. We spent the rest of the day unpacking, draping things out to air, and arranging our tents.

Mick, famous for his preference for the old and worn, "tried and trusted is best", always kept his ice-climbing gear ready packed in a patched Outward Bound rucksack, which lived in his kitchen. But for this trip he had also acquired a brand new Berghaus Expedition eighty-litre sack. This object had useful tightening straps on the sides, three to a side; three more straps across the back; adjustable straps on the lid; a structural harness with two pairs of straps and buckles; and a complicated size-adjusting system to accommodate a range of back sizes. To obtain the best performance from the sack was like solving a three dimensional IQ test.

Mick spent the rest of the afternoon failing the test, and complaining to Chris about "ridiculous modern gear". He was of course complaining to the wrong person. As manager of Alpine Sports, Chris was nothing less than a fully certified gear freak.

"It's a prototype Berghaus are working on," Chris held out his Gore-tex jacket, "it's based on the Gemini, but it's got this zip-on full storm hood from the Kang, and extra long sleeves . . . "

"'Cos they think you're an ape." Mick's contribution was firmly ignored by Chris.

" . . . and I've got them to simplify the inner jacket to reduce weight, using a Libond filling . . . "

"What's Libond?" I asked foolishly.

"Ah, Libond is . . . " Chris went on for quite a while and I don't remember any of it. Meanwhile Mick had returned to his rucksack armed with one of Dai's kitchen knives, and a wicked vengeful look in his eye. He was going to cut off every damned strap he could lay his hands on, and make the Berghaus Expedition resemble a tried-and-trusted Outward Bound as closely as possible.

The next day we started on our first task, to understand the shape of the mountain, and plan a route on it. Mick and I crossed the Lower Ultar Glacier with Hassan, and climbed a ridge to a notch at about 14,000 feet. From there we could survey the entire DP Bowl, and the West Ridge as far as the West Col. Mick found himself unaccountably drawn towards the DP Pillar, he plotted a route up it, a gully here, a difficult rock step there, leading to a narrow ice ramp and so on.

"It's easy when you pick the right line, know what I mean?"

Mick was so convincing that even I began to think, momentarily, that it might make a reasonable route, until Hassan pointed out the line of the Japanese attempt two years earlier. Now that looked like a line. It was perhaps even the sort of line I might attempt. Straight up the slope below the West Col and trot along the West Ridge. The reconnaissance was over. Mick and Hassan sat back in a thyme bush, clouds of aromatic dust enveloped them, as they pulled out their chapatis and biscuits. Below us, the sun-baked glacier was spread out like a model landscape.

"So," I said between mouthfuls, "you and Watty will try that pillar . . . hmmm, I think the B-team are going to have a go at the col and ridge. By the way, Hassan, why did the Japanese not finish the route?" Hassan pointed out a prominent rock buttress which barred the way to the West Ridge.

"The rock is very steep. They could not pass it."

"Oh dear," I thought," here we go again."

5

When Mick, Hassan and I got back to Base it was almost dark. The kitchen now sported a three-foot loose stone wall, buttressed with sacks of rice and potatoes. The team were spread out in the gloom of the awning with tin plates on their knees, and were prodding the contents listlessly. Dai had made a pot of wet rice, and the first of a truly dismal series of curries. This time it was dhal, flavoured only with chilli powder.

"Oh well," I said, "at least we've got a sports plan. Only thing is how to get to the Hunza Glacier."

"There's a barrier about an hour above us," said Boydie. "There's a ravine, and a cliff on the far side. We went up the ravine a bit, it's on snow. It doesn't look good."

"Any chance of getting Dai to cook boiled potatoes next time?" interrupted George. "I can't eat any of this ghee stuff and raw chilli."

I realised that I too had not actually swallowed any of the food. I could see that life at Base was not going to be perfect.

Phil was the only one who seemed to be enjoying his supper. He held out his plate for more, and said that he had examined another gully, which he had followed for several hundred feet and drawn a blank, ending up tip-toeing across a tiny ledge above a roaring ravine.

"I was talking to the shepherd," continued Boydie, while secretly trying to dispose of his food behind the rice sacks, "and he says there is a way through the cliff, right where it looks impossible."

The evening drew on and one by one we retired to our tents. The night was clear, and Phil set up a tripod and took a long moonlit exposure of the mountain. John and Boydie, plugged into their respective Walkmans, lay encased in their expedition sleeping bags. Snatches of conversation, gossip and unlikely stories wafted on the breeze from Mick and Chris's tent. Liaquat had found the expedition booze supply, and was testing it alone in his tunnel tent. George and Steve and Dai had long since fallen asleep. I read and re-read the first page of *Gravity's Rainbow*, unaware that I had not taken it in. The mountain growled, distant séracs collapsed and crumpled onto unseen glaciers. The dream world was here and sleep soon followed.

I was paired to climb with Phil Butler, whom we all called Lobby. This name was the result of an incident in Scotland involving a ceilidh in Kinlochleven, half the Bojohaghur team and several lobster pots. It was the club practice when climbing in Scotland to doss in any old uninhabited shelter, and we found a creosoted timber shed filled with fishing equipment. One wall was stacked ceiling high with lobster pots, and hanging from each one was a length of bright blue polypropylene rope. More coils of the blue rope lined the other walls of the shed, but there was just about enough room for us to spread our sleeping bags. Most people find a good deal of whisky induces a catatonic state, and so did three of us. But Phil performed an extended zombie dance that night, unconscious that he was jumping on us, pulling at the lobster pots, and all the while crying aloud, "It's so blue . . . My God, it is so very blue. This is the bluest blue I have ever seen." We woke in the morning to find the entire wall of pots had fallen over us. We had to tunnel our way out, and on top of the pots there was a snoring Phil Butler. A new Phil Butler had been revealed to us. Till now we had considered him the very model of self-control, and for a while, to commemorate the discovery, we referred to Blue Lobsters when talking of Phil, which in time reduced itself to to its present diminutive.

Phil and I sat on a boulder near Boydie's ravine, searching the cliffs for the Boydie route. It was already early afternoon, and the others had gone ahead. Phil and I had spent the day organising our tent, sorting out climbing gear, food and clothes. But we could not work out where the others had gone. There was no apparent line of weakness. We had just agreed to look for an alternative route, when Phil said, "Look!" There was a line of goats on the cliff! They were strung out in a straight line diagonally across the rock, and there behind them came the shepherd, carrying a kid across his shoulders. I rubbed my eyes, and looked again, but the flock was still there. A few minutes later they overran us. The goats seemed very keen to nibble our rucksacks which we held aloft, thereby exposing our nobbly knees and hairy calves. In a way, this was worse. The goats suddenly became very interested in our sun cream, and proceeded to lick the cream off our legs. This was particularly bad news for me, I have always been seriously allergic to most animals. As the rough goat tongues scraped and slobbered down the back of my legs, I began to sneeze. I was horrified, surely I would now develop a rash. I would be unable to bend the legs. I might not be able to climb for ages. I desperately needed to run away. But, some of the goats had three horns, so running away might be exceedingly dangerous. I could feel an attack of panic-induced asthma growing.

We were rescued when the shepherd, guffawing at our ineptitude, booted his animals out of the way. He was only four feet tall, he wore cut down wellington boots with no socks, his skin was like old bark, and he had only two teeth when he smiled. But the real shock, as he unslung the kid from his narrow shoulders, was his apparent age. The man looked at least eighty years old. So perhaps there was some truth in those stories about

Hunza longevity.

We walked up to the ravine following the hoof prints, and the shepherd's gesticulated directions, and there we could see a definite, though frightening, ramp across the cliff. It was not hard, yet I needed both hands to hold on. I could not imagine how the ancient shepherd had sauntered down the ramp so easily. Above Boydie's ravine, easy slabs and steep meadows led in about one and a half hours to the next major obstacle, the Ring.

It was on the last of the meadows before the Ring that we found the others, and the excavations of the Japanese expedition. The Japanese had constructed several flat platforms for their tents, and called this place Advance Base Camp. We did likewise. If Base was attractively remote from the mountain, Advance Base was morbidly intimate. The place was overhung by enormous granite walls, nearby the leering icefalls and séracs of the Ring dribbled stones and boulders of all sizes. There appeared to be no safe way to the upper glaciers. One of the reasons the Japanese had failed, said Hassan, was that every member of the party suffered some kind of injury from stonefall. From Advance Base we could see why.

"What time did they start climbing every day?" we had asked Hassan.

"Eight, maybe nine o'clock."

"Ah!" we said.

It was obvious that night climbing was the only way to avoid injury, always assuming, of course, that we could find a practical route through to the glaciers. There was a route, and the A-team found it.

Just above Advance Base, a torrent sprang from a hole in the side of séracs, and cascaded down a steep narrow ravine. The ravine ended abruptly, creating a small waterfall on the left of the Ring. Mick and Chris found that it was possible to cross this ravine at night and, on the far side, a buttress of ice-polished granite slabs led to a thinning in the Ring séracs. There was an easyish gully behind one of the giant ice blocks and, provided that block did not slide down the slabs while we were there, we would have no problem gaining the glaciers above the Ring. The main danger was the narrow ravine. As soon as the sun fell on the glaciers, the ravine became like a rifle range. Fusillades of stones and gravel ricocheted through the gully. This was one place that we marked down as night-time-only country.

We had carried up climbing gear, sleeping bags and some food, but no tent during that two-night reconnaissance, and it rained both nights. We were very wet and muddy when we decided to return to Base, where George was still complaining about the food. Apparently Dai had boiled his potatoes with chilli for breakfast. George had now identified four elements of Dai's cooking which he found unpalatable: ghee, dhal, chillis and rice. Unfortunately for George, these elements were, in varying proportions, the sole ingredients for most of Dai's dishes. Dai meanwhile had discovered that he was feeling too ill to carry out his part of the bargain, bringing fresh vegetables from Baltit. He had a stomach ache, and after a day at Base, so did I.

The next day, as a rest cure, I thought it would be sensible to carry a tent and food to Advance Base. We should be able to do our own cooking there. Mick and Chris had left early in the morning, and John and Boydie would join us at Advance Base in the evening. George and Steve, our trekker, were going to climb the ridge above Base, taking a picnic. Liaquat had begun a series of conversations with Dai which proceeded over endless cups of tea.

Over the next three days Phil and I explored the lower part of the route. We followed the A-team line across the Dangerous Ravine, hopping from boulder to boulder, and checking the fountain spouting from the sérac for stonefall. Mick and Chris had left a 7-mm line hanging down the polished slabs, which we tied onto thankfully. There

was no belay, and dawn was bringing a growing aware-
ness of the nasty drop below. But our peace of mind was
illusory, for the top of the line was tied round an ice
pinnacle, which was beginning to lean downhill.

The pressure of the two large glaciers converging on the
Ring crumpled the ice into the strangest landscape, waves
of ice a hundred feet high, zones of crushed blocks, can-
yons, alleys, arching bridges, all perched on the edge of
the Ring. For us it was an intricate maze that was never
the same shape twice. Mick had built cairns, but even
after twenty-four hours many of them had lost their balance on the shifting glacier.

We needed to escape from the maze to gain the Hunza
Glacier. Standing on the heights of one pressure wave
Phil said that he could see Mick and Chris moving very
slowly across the entrance to DP Valley. A little more
surveying revealed an unusual ice valley to our right
which marked the junction of the two glaciers above the
Ring. We followed this and, turning left at the far end,
realised quite suddenly that we had finished with the first
section of our route. It had taken us four hours. Three
hours later we had climbed the Hunza Glacier by its left
bank, and found a boulder the size of a bungalow to
bivouac under, the Flat Boulder Bivouac. Soon we were
joined by Mike and John. The four of us sat out in the
evening sun and I put some gravelly water on my stove.
As usual I could not get the thing going.

"Here, Lobby, you're the technical one, you try."

"Okay. There, easy as that . . . Hey, look!" Phil was
pointing at a billowing powder avalanche on the far side
of the mountain. We watched as the white cloud spread
out to fill the entire DP Valley. Phil stirred a sachet of
Ovaltine into the tepid glacier water, and said, "I hope
Mick and Watty aren't in the middle of that. It's filled in
all the crevasses they were avoiding."

By then Mick and Chris Watts had crossed the entrance
to DP valley, and dug a snow hole on the far side.

Mick told us later, "Watty was feeling really ill, groaning and so on. The snow hole was just above the bergschrund, so I climbed up to some rocks above. It wasn't hard, just scrambling, when there was this mega-rumbling. I thought, effing hell! I mean it was monstrous, I didn't think I was going to die, but it looked very unpleasant, so I tried to run up the hill to escape. But that didn't work very well, and when I looked back it was obvious that I couldn't get out that way, so I jumped down behind this flake of rock, a kind of rock crevasse. Then it came over and snowed really hard for a minute. But Watty didn't know what was going on, the sky just went black and some of the gear lying in front of the snow hole blew away."

The next stage of our own route was the Three Thousand Foot Slope, which led directly to the West Col. The structure of this feature was relatively simple. After a broad and deep bergschrund that guarded almost the entire slope, there was a lower face and an upper face, separated by a band of steep rocks that were penetrated by ice-filled gullies. The day after the DP avalanche, the four of us started out for the right-hand of the face, where an avalanche had bridged the bergschrund. It was dark, and we crossed the glacier below the slope at our own pace, Phil racing ahead, then Boydie, John and last, me. Boydie had a sudden attack of stomach pains, and turned back after twenty minutes, and John, worried about Boydie, went back with him. I would have returned too, but Phil had my stove and food, and by now he was out of earshot. His headtorch darted like a firefly up and down the slope, as he picked a route towards the bergschrund, where he waited for me. We climbed eight or nine pitches before midday, when the sun put a temporary halt to progress. The snow had softened to the consistency of porridge, and was almost thigh-deep in some places. But we had passed the lower face and were able to find a satisfyingly flat ledge on a crumbly ridge that stuck out from the slope like a long black whaleback.

Evidently the Japanese had passed the same way, there were remains of bleached polypropylene rope. We placed a few pegs of our own, and dug the stove out of the rucksack. It was lunch time. It was great to be on a Karakoram face again. We were at about 18,000 feet, looking down towards our base 6500 feet below. The depths where the Hunza river ran were dark, and on the far side of the Hunza the valley systems that made up the Mirdom of Nagar nestled under the white masses of Diran and Rakaposhi, and their outliers. A spectacular V-shaped gorge pointed straight at Diran, while in the haze, there was something menacing on the horizon, a shining prow that was to appear to me in dreams – Spantik.

Above us there appeared to be a choice of lines. To the right, mixed ground with ice-filled gullies led shortly to a long snow or ice field below the West Col. To the left, a single steep icefall gave access to a broadening couloir which finished to the left of the West Col. Hassan said the Japanese had taken the left-hand route, so after lunch Phil and I climbed three pitches on snow to the bottom of the icefall. It was about 120 feet high, and very nearly vertical.

"The Japanese must have been very good to get up this," Phil said.

"I don't think they did," I replied. "You'd expect to find fixed rope in a place like this, and even if it had been torn away by avalanches, there should be bits of it around. But there's not even any sign of bolts or pegs. Hassan was wrong."

"He's been right about everything else so far," said Phil. It was typical of him to defend Hassan because he was not there. "And he said he had been this far with the Japanese."

"Well, he obviously had not."

It was now late afternoon. We decided to bivouac where we were, under the shelter of the buttress bounding the right side of the icefall. It was quick work cutting a ledge out of the snow, and after half an hour, we happily hung our bivi tent, the same one I had used on Uzum Brakk, loosely over our heads. The afternoon heat brought avalanches of porridge, slurrying over the icefall, and a fine veil of fog that enveloped us in a beguiling, comforting softness. It began to snow very gently. Phil put on yet another brew. The stove purred under Phil's mechanical hands. Then there was another noise in the white fastness, a kind of moan. Phil cocked his head on one side.

"Victor ... Lobby ... " the wailing sound seemed to say.

"I think someone is calling us."

"Impossible."

"Victor ... Lobby ... " the moaning went on.

"It *is* some one, you know. Hello-oh ... hell-oh ... Who ... is ... it?"

"It's meeeee ... "

"Oh, that is useful," said Phil.

"It's me, Mick."

"Where ... are ... you?"

"About 600 feet ... below you ... I am alone."

"What ... the ... hell ... are ... you ... doing?"

"Have ... you ... got ... any ... water?"

"Whaaat?"

"Water?"

"Why ... do ... you ... want ... water?"

"I have ... forgotten ... my pot ... I have got ... the stove ... but I've forgotten ... the ... pot ... I am ... parched."

"Use ... something ... else," I said, thinking of a foil packet, or an empty gas canister.

"I ... tried ... using ... my ... helmet ... but ... it ... burns."

"We ... can't ... help ... you," shouted Phil, and added for my benefit, "We can't help him because he is completely stark staring bonkers."

In the morning it was still dark and cold when Phil and I started down. The snow which had been like wet concrete the afternoon before had now set. When we reached the whaleback ridge Mick had gone, but his signature was there. A scattering of uncomfortable stones, a scrap of Mars bar wrapper, a few matches and a charred puddle of melted plastic showed he had bivouacked where Phil and I had stopped for lunch. At the base of the Three Thousand Foot Slope, Chris had met up with John and Boydie at the Flat Boulder Bivouac. While Mick was busy boiling his helmet, they had started down, leaving a cache of gear and food, and descending to the Ring, where the expedition suffered its first casualty. John's crampons broke and he fell twenty feet while traversing into the ice valley, from a sérac wall, landing on his back. He was in a certain amount of pain, and complained that Chris and Mike forced him to continue the long and devious Ring crossing. They had no choice. It was imperative to get him off the glacier. (Later X-rays showed that he had broken his back in two places.)

Phil and I caught up with John at our Advance Base, where he had been left by the others. We asked him how he felt.

"Just bruised. I'll be all right."

But he could hardly move from his sleeping bag. Phil stopped to look after him, while I went on down to Base. I left my climbing gear, duvet jacket and salopettes behind and, with only a sleeping bag and Karrimat in the rucksack, I ran down the steep meadows. I was looking forward to the peace and quiet of Base.

"Hello, Dai, get a brew on," I shouted as I ran round the bend of the last bit of goat track. There was no response, I shouted again, but only attracted the attentions of a few curious goats. When I reached the kitchen it was clear that all was not well.

George was refusing to eat any more food at Base. "Chillies . . . yech, ghee . . . urghh, dhal . . . yeurgh."

Liaquat and Dai's conversation had evolved into open argument. It was time for another carry from Baltit. We needed fuel, vegetables and eggs. Liaquat was insisting that Dai should pop down to Baltit for the day, but Dai would not go. Not without the instructions of the leader . . . so I asked him. But it was clear that our poor cook was suffering a major attack of hypochondria. This time it was his back.

"That's okay," I said, "we'll go down for you, I could do with a good meal at Kalb Ali's. Do you think you'll be all right on your own, Dai?" Dai sadly nodded his head and clutched his side. "I think so, but please bring medicine."

Liaquat walked down to Baltit with us. He was no longer on speaking terms with Dai and insisted on climbing with us. He showed me the rule book, and a sheaf of Roneoed brown papers, the government regulations.

"See, it is here. The LO shall accompany the expedition to a high point."

"Well, Liaquat, your high point is going to be Advance Base. I am not going to be responsible for you on the glacier," I said.

"If you do not climb with me, I shall go alone, and climb the mountain."

"Liaquat, listen to me carefully. You are not competent to set foot on the glacier."

I made two mistakes with this intemperate outburst. First of all, Liaquat refused to speak to me again, and this made the running of the expedition rather complicated. John, who had managed not to inflame our liaison officer, had to act as interlocutor. The second mistake was that I was hardly the best judge of competence.

Two days later the remaining five healthy team members left for Advance Base. As I meandered up last, I could not help noticing that the others were not making my brew. In fact they were wandering about the hillside.

"Hey, Victor, the tent's gone."

"What?"

"The tent's gone. Can you see the fly-sheet anywhere?"

"What on earth are you wittering on about? Who can have possibly taken our . . . " and at that point I began to understand. "Crikey, it must have been an enormous one."

Our belongings were scattered, Mike's helmet had disappeared completely, and the goats had added to the damage, eating whole packets of soups, chocolate and porridge, wrapping and all. They had even eaten the leather straps from my climbing helmet. But there was worse.

"The animals, the bloody animals," I shouted. "They've peeed all over my duvet and salopettes."

Friends? What kind of friends are they that can only laugh at your misfortune.

6

Dawn. A slight diabatic breeze drifted down the slope, but not strongly enough to suppress the odour of goat urine which wafted from my salopettes with each movement. We were moving slowly. For once, I was in front.

"Can't you try and stop smelling?" Phil asked, somewhat unreasonably, I thought.

"What you do . . . is pace yourself, you see." I decided to ignore the man. Phil grunted, so I went on. "Don't take a step . . . unless you feel ready . . . to take the next one too." Swing the tools. Left axe, swing thump, right axe, swing thump, left boot, kick, right boot, crunch . . . rest, breathe, go . . . left axe, thump, right axe thump, left boot kick, right boot kick . . . rest, breathe . . . Our conversation followed the rhythm of the climbing. "Rest at each move . . . that way you don't stop. It's all in the pacing." I do tend to go on a bit at times.

"But it doesn't help, does it?"

"Eh? Help with what?"

"The 'orrible smell."

The thin light showed how high we had climbed. Phil and I were nearing the top of the Three Thousand Foot Slope. Below us, following in our track, were Mick and Chris. The layer of snow covering the slope had thinned progressively as we gained height, and now we were beginning to climb on bare ice. We had been climbing unroped till now, but balancing on the tips of our frontpoints was tiring. I stopped to belay, and Phil led through.

Ninety feet above, he climbed onto the only feature on the upper slope. It was a slab of granite, sticking straight out of the slope like a bracket. From below, it looked dangerously unstable. Phil placed two screws above the slab, and we started to cut away the ice to expose a reasonably flat ledge, about the size of a double bed. The Japanese had clearly passed this way, we uncovered a roll of Karrimat and an oxygen mask.

"Asthmatics?" suggested Phil.

It was now 8.00 am. The Himalayan sun was already in energy-draining mode. I did not envy Mick and Chris, who were still some way below. Mick arrived at 9.00 am just in time for tea. Chris had been caught out by the sun, and slowed right down. In the end we brought him up on a rope. The effect of mountain sun is peculiar. It is not the heat alone that drains energy, it is quite possible to perform fairly energetic feats in the sun, even at quite high altitudes. The really enervating thing is the combination of heat, light and snow. The reflected rays on a glacier or snow slope have an effect like a microwave oven. It seems to cook you right through to the core. In addition, the rays penetrate the snow and soften it to a depth of feet which adds to the difficulty of daytime movement. In the Karakoram this effect seems to lessen at about 21,000 feet, where the daytime temperature drops sufficiently to remove one factor from the equation. We were now at about 19,500 feet, roughly 6000 metres.

That night we found ourselves trying to fit our rucksacks, cooking equipment and bodies onto the slab. There was not enough space for four. Phil slept sitting up. I draped my left side over a belay rope. Chris found that he could rest at the tip of the slab, with Mick's legs piled on top of him. We were all belayed back to Phil's two ice screws. It was so uncomfortable that we had to take sleeping pills to doze off, and perhaps this had something to do with what happened next.

Chris was held in balance by the weight of Mick's legs.

During the night Mick rolled over, releasing Chris, who was catapulted out into space. We all woke with a start, not least, Chris Watts. Because I was draped round the belay ropes, which suddenly became bar tight, I thought someone was trying to strangle me.

"Whaa . . . ?"

"Chrissake, what's going on?"

"Why are the ropes so tight?"

"Where's Watty?"

Someone managed to switch a headtorch on.

"Oh no, Watty's fallen off."

"Oh . . . shit . . . oh . . . no."

"God, this is desperate . . . "

Just at that moment there was a call. It was a muffled wailing sound, coming from under the slab. Cautiously Mick peered over the edge. There was a sleeping bag suspended from a single rope, slowly rotating in the beam of the torch like a giant cocoon. Chris was dangling over a 3000-foot drop. It was from the bag, which had closed up over his head, that the wailing noise emanated.

"What's he saying, Mick?"

"He wants some jumars."

"Is he hurt?"

"No. He says he is totally untouched, and can he have those jumars."

"There's much more space here now. Can't he wait there till dawn?" Even Phil nodded at this suggestion.

"He says *no* . . . and stop arsing about."

Chris jumared up without leaving his sleeping bag, but on the way up, his jacket, the wonderful prototype Gemini, began to detach itself. It had been pinned against the rock by Chris's rope. Even as Chris reached out to save the jacket, his own movement released it into the darkness. I am not sure, but I believe I heard a modest cough of approval from Mick's direction.

Dawn was a long time coming. When it arrived we found all that remained of Chris's boots were the zip tags, carefully tied into the ropes. By a miracle, one of the boots was entangled in the ropes under the slab. But the other was gone. We took stock of our situation. Chris would have to go down, and Mick would help him. There was the Japanese Karrimat, and I had a roll of sticky tape. With a little creative cordwaining, we constructed a makeshift foam shell over which Chris strapped his crampons. It took Mick and Chris three days to descend to Base. Mick later wrote of the descent:

Things started as I hoped they would not continue. Two diagonal abseils meant strain on the Karrimat foot crampon, which promptly twisted round to point meaningfully at the sky. Progress continued haltingly as Watty kept on course by way of a sequence of athletic hops. Above, Vic and Lob could be seen disappearing into the first of a series of worrying-looking clouds.

A Japanese snowshoe protruding from the slope proved to be of some assistance on the boot front. Although large and clumsy, it sported two spikes of a sort. Watty cut up some more Karrimat. The snowshoe was strapped in place and the Mark 2 Boot was in use. The improvements over Mark 1 were marginal and by darkness we were still well above our bivi spot with no ledge in sight.

A night perched on a protruding flake in continuing snow did little to inspire enthusiasm for the day ahead, but with Watty becoming a hopping expert, progress was slightly faster and, despite a time-consuming rope jam, mid-afternoon saw us back on the infamous helmet boiling bivi.

The descent continued interminably. Unfortunately the easiest way down the icefall necessitated climbing up and down several vertical ice walls, an activity which was somewhat problematic when hindered by a snowshoe and general exhaustion. But with minimal ropework we left the glacier by late afternoon and by darkness the Mark 3 Karrimat Boot was arriving at Base Camp.

Phil and I, meanwhile, went on. This was probably a mistake, and we should have retreated after Mick and Chris. But we were not yet blessed with hindsight. Bojohaghur's West Col (now rechristened Dangle Col) was just half a pitch above the scene of Watts' Dangle. The bivouac looked incredibly exposed. I stopped to take a photograph, and wave at Chris and Mick. From the col the West Wall of the Batura Group and East Face of Sangamarmar faced each other across the deep Hassanabad Glacier. Looking westwards, we could see that the beautiful Hunza Peak culminated in a crest of oversailing snow mushrooms and séracs, waves of ice about to break over the face. Our route now turned eastwards, we were finally on Bojohaghur's West Ridge, and we intended to follow this to the summit. The ridge had looked fairly difficult from below. Above Dangle Col there appeared to be a 1300-foot buttress of steep, smooth granite. Hassan had said the Japanese were halted by the buttress, so for three days and 8000 feet, Phil and I had carried an extra rope, half a dozen rock pegs and some wired nuts, in addition to the ice-climbing gear, which we knew we would need anyway.

Perhaps the Japanese had not been accurately translated, or Hassan was wrong. The rock buttress could be avoided on its left, via an icefield that did not exceed sixty degrees but proved to be tiring. The repetitive movement onto the crampon front points under the burden of the oversize rucksacks strained the calf muscles, and with each upward swing of an axe, our shoulders lifted the entire twenty-kilo load. We were becoming tired.

Clouds, which had earlier been flirting with the neighbouring peaks, blew half gales around the buttress, the gathering snow slithered off the ice in waves of spindrift. Our buttress was capped by a broad low-angled shoulder, which we followed in the deteriorating weather. The drifting snow was now needle sharp. We needed to escape the weather. It was early afternoon when Phil stumbled into a hole in the ice. He had discovered a crevasse which sloped in at right angles from the face. It was a sort of bergschrund with no apparent reason to be there. We hung our rucksacks from screws near the hole and squeezed ourselves in. We were out of the wind. The ice shelved down awkwardly and the low ceiling was hung with spicules and fronds which broke off to produce a chiming tinkling accompaniment to each movement.

"Do you want to bivi here?" I asked Phil.

"It's bloody cold. Look, the ice is like steel."

"But no wind, should be the best place in a storm."

"Let's come back when there is a storm, then."

Breath-clouds measured the sentences. I hesitated, I liked the eerie atmosphere.

"Come on, Victor. This is a deathtrap."

"Oh all right . . . grumble . . . grumble."

We had to crawl out of the tiny entrance into a minor maelstrom. But I had to admit, it was warmer. Two pitches later a rock buttress loomed out of the mist. It was to provide two small ledges, one for each of us. Phil had the slightly larger ledge, so he made the brews, and lowered them in the pot by rope. We made up small quantities of Cadbury's Smash, and had an inch of Negroni Milano salami each. The Milano is a fine grained and lightly peppered sausage, ideal for bivouacs. We also experimented with the Napoli, but the coarse texture seems to make it less palatable on the mountain. The lumps of fat, so full of essential energy, got stuck between the teeth. Perhaps chewing Napoli is simply too much effort at altitude.

We had plenty of time to discuss the niceties of the choice of salami, because we became storm-bound at this bivouac site for three nights. During this time, I began to suffer from headaches, which I took to be incipient altitude sickness. John had provided us with a supply of DF 118, which he said was some kind of opiate. I took quite a lot of those, with no effect on my headache. But John forgot to say that DF 118 was also an anti-diarrhoeal, so it gave me chronic constipation, which lasted for days. Meanwhile the migraine symptoms roared on. Phil helped by massaging my neck, which was delightful while he worked on the joints. I read *The Man from Saint Petersburg* and then Marco Polo's *Travels*. Sometimes *The Travels* seemed more real than our own situation, sometimes it was difficult to strip away the onion-skin layers of fantasies, to reveal the one we were inhabiting. My head hurt, for three days the storms and the headaches beat like angry fists on my eggshell universe.

On the third morning I told Phil I was too ill to continue. Phil cooked porridge and tea, we ate in a state of depression. As we packed our sacks, the wind, which had now dropped to a gentle breeze, picked up Phil's Karrimat. He looked on impotently as it floated down into the valley. Were the ancient worshippers of Bon-Po right? Are there really gods of place, of stream and mountain? Perhaps for us there was some pristine deity awaiting the sacrifice of one Karrimat. Because, no sooner had it slipped away into the cloud-filled valleys, than the same clouds rolled away. As the mountain unravelled itself from the remaining wisps, we could see the clear dark blue sky stretching away to the horizon. This was the morning after the storm. The West Ridge lay before us.

"Come on, Lobby, it's your pitch."

"What about your head?"

"Ignore it, we can't waste the weather. This could be our only good spell all summer . . . and you can share my Karrimat." I had already uncoiled the rope, and was flicking the end at Phil.

My headaches dissipated after the first pitch of the day. They never returned, and I was left wondering whether the entire attack of migraine had been just another episode of hypochondria. I find it harder and harder to tell as I grow older. The theory I formed during the morning's climbing was that, depressed by the very real external threats, my tired old office-worker's body had creatively occupied itself, devising valid excuses for descent which the mind could not reject.

From Watts' Dangle, at about 19,500 feet, the West Ridge rose steeply to the first intermediary peak at 22,900 feet. From there, the ridge varied less in vertical interval, and over about two miles rose only another thousand feet, taking in one more peak on the way to the summit. From our bivouac the shoulder narrowed into a graceful ice arête which soared for several pitches to the base of a battery of large séracs guarding the first peaks of the ridge. As we gained height it became clear that the ice arête led to a dead end. It finished under at least eighty feet of overhanging ice. Phil and I argued about which line looked the least unpleasant, but neither of us could actually see enough to judge by. We chose to turn the first sérac on its right. After midday it began snowing again, so we excavated a miserable snow hole under the overhanging ice. Initially we stopped for a brew, but the snow fell more thickly, and there was no point in moving when we did not know where to go. Our snow hole had a gap in the back, which connected it to a crevasse. The gap let out a steady draft of super-cooled air. Somehow the atmosphere managed to be damp as well as freezing. Phil refused to share my Karrimat, preferring to lie on the rope.

The next morning we started late, as is normal after a miserable bivouac. There was more argument and general confusion about what line to take through the séracs. But this was enjoyable, mountaineering as route-finding, and there is no more enjoyable route-finding than new route-finding. The key turned out to be a full pitch of perfectly flat, steel-hard ice, about seventy degrees. Very tiring with our blunt crampons and even blunter axes not biting properly. Phil was belayed to a pair of solid screws, his huge rucksack dangling below, to take the weight off his shoulders.

"Superb lead, Lob." I meant it. It is no mean thing to balance up 150 feet of steep brittle ice on the tips of your crampons under the burden of a heavy rucksack. "Which way now?"

"It might be possible to get under that cornice on the left."

"Okay, but watch the rope. The cornice looks awfully fragile."

The cornice curled into a tube, which I crawled into. The far end of the tube opened onto a ledge, and suddenly I realised I was on flat ground.

"Hey, Lobster, we've cracked it! whoopeee . . . "

The weather closed in soon after Phil joined me. We had no choice but to take an early bivouac. We needed visibility more than anything else, and the problem with bad weather is that it can obscure easy climbing more thoroughly than technically difficult routes. On hard climbs, there is often an obvious feature, an overhanging crack or corner, perhaps, that leads you on, and provides a shadow looming through the mists. But the main danger on this snow-covered ground was hidden crevasses, and the cloud made everything equally white. There is no horizon, no visual clue. Up could be anywhere. So could down.

Our ninth day on the climb brought easy climbing and more wind, clouds and snow. We sighted our route in glimpses during brief cloud clearances. We climbed on into the clouds. The wind began to pick up the loose snow and spit it into our faces. By late morning Phil and I were strung out along the top of an enormous icecream roll in the middle of an electrical storm. Bright flashes of light illuminated the mountainscape.

Things are beginning to look distinctly ugly, I thought. Through the gloom, I could see Phil jerking about like a puppet in spasms. It took some time before I understood he was being played on by the static electricity. And it would soon be my turn.

"Down . . . croak . . . get down, Lobby!" I could only manage a hoarse whisper into the wind. God, what a time to lose your voice.

I lay down in the snow, cowering, and pulled my rucksack over my head. As if that could do anything for me. I must have been an ostrich in a previous life. It didn't help. In seconds the first invisible stabs reached my end of the rope. Gasping with fright, I unclipped the ice screws and karabiners from my waist and, clipping them into a long sling, hurled them away from me. Next I took my ice axes, and threw them as far as their slings would allow. I pushed my boots into the snow to try and bury the crampon points. I really did not want to become a lightning conductor. On the neighbouring peaks the lightning flashed and boomed.

"Any moment . . . any moment now . . . " I knew then what it was to be a mouse teased by a cat. The world seemed likely to end with both a bang and a whimper. I supplied the whimpering.

After about twenty minutes of this it became clear to me that my time had not yet come after all. Lightning was still striking the peaks across the valley as, with fumbling urgency, Phil and I crawled down the side of the icecream roll, and into a snow bowl under the roll of the cornice. Now we were out of danger, but the snow bowl was the permanent home of a howling gale. We would have to dig out a snow hole or freeze. I had carried up a lightweight shovel specially for the purpose and Phil, being the craftsman, took charge of digging operations. It was still early in the day, and he had time to create an enormous cavern, while I brewed tea and admired his boundless energy. Anyway, I am more neurotic than Phil, so had probably found the entire electric episode more emotionally draining than he had. This justified our roles, I reasoned.

Inside the snow hole we could stand, slightly bent over, and there were two bunks and a trench to catch the cold air, a shelf for a candle, and a solid table for cooking on. We were completely insulated from the weather, a cosy light filtered through the outer wall. There was no wind noise. That night we took stock. The snow cave was close to 7000 metres. We had food for two more days, and there was some more food left behind by Mick and Chris at Watts' Dangle. We had enough gas to melt snow for perhaps seven days. It had taken us nine days to get here, of which three full days, and two half days had been spent sitting out bad weather. So, five days up. It was too cold outside to climb in the dark, or in high wind. We wore our down jackets continually. Our sleeping bags had by now lost their insulation, doubling their weight and halving their size through condensation. Some Americans have experimented with a vapour barrier bag inside their sleeping bag, which is nothing more than a polythene bag, but the technique has yet to catch on in Europe. We suffered chronically from cold feet. Often we could feel nothing at all from the ankle down. We had acquired the latest model of Koflaks, with Aveolite inners (as recommended by Chris), but still the only sign of life from our toes was the pain as they warmed up from time to time. Phil took Ronicol every morning. I took it occasionally, but that did not make any difference either. It was Phil who eventually contracted mild frostbite. Perhaps our metabolism had sunk so low as a result of the low oxygen pressure and the starvation diet, that the body could no longer generate enough natural heat to keep the extremities warm. And Phil, of course, had no Karrimat. Without insulation from the snow, he was losing energy just lying down.

We had overslept. I sat up with a start and banged my head on the low ceiling, showers of snow everywhere. Leaning over, I pulled the rucksack out of the wall. Through the hole we could see the grey dawn light change hue, growing into a warm pink. It was a beautiful colour. Phil began the task of squeezing his swollen feet into his boots. I brewed tea and weak porridge.

"Great, eh. Just one big push."

Phil was silent.

"We'll leave the books here, and some gas. How much have we got?"

"Seven cylinders," said Phil.

"Shall we take two with us, and leave the rest?"

"Think that's enough?"

"Yup, and the shovel, mark the entrance to the snow hole with it?"

"Okay but we'd better not leave anything too important here."

"Why?"

"Case we can't find it in bad weather."

"It's going to be okay, Lob, we're doing well."

We left the snow cave and laboriously reclimbed the giant icecream roll. By 9.00 am we had reached the top of the roll, and could see that we had in fact reached the first of the peaks on the West Ridge. Before us lay the second peak, and somewhere behind that, the main summit. The face before us looked impressive. It was wedge-shaped, and at an apparently easy angle. It could not have been more than a thousand feet high, but seen all at once, it looked enormous. Below the face lay an easy snow saddle.

"It's easy. It's really straight forward," I said. "From the saddle it will be just plodding, the only thing that can stop us now is snow conditions, Lob."

But we could not get off the icecream roll. First Phil tried to walk down to the snow saddle and came back, shaking his head. "It won't go."

I could not believe my eyes, the saddle was only 300 feet from us. I tried. Phil was right. I still could not believe it. The Giant Icecream Roll overhung, like a mushroom, on all sides but the one we had climbed up. Even if we could abseil down to the saddle, we would not be able to climb back up. What we needed was a clearly reversible route to the saddle. Anything else would be courting disaster, climbing into an irreversible situation.

"Only thing I can suggest is trying to traverse under the saddle from the Snow Bowl."

Phil looked blankly at me. He seemed suddenly very very tired.

We retraced our steps to the Snow Bowl. Phil took a belay on the edge of the bowl. Clanking with ice screws and pegs, I stepped out into space. Steep glassy ice, plunging 6500 feet down to the Hassanabad Glacier.

"It's fantastic, Lobby, pant . . . puff . . . it's real climbing," I shouted. Next there was a section of granite blocks laced with iced cracks, and perfect peg placements. "It's just like the Dubh Loch."

In Scotland, at Craig an Dubh Loch, the pitch might have taken fifteen minutes. Here 160 feet took an hour. "On . . . belay," I shouted.

Phil spent about fifteen minutes starting the pitch and then returned to the edge of the Snow Bowl.

"Come on, Lobby, it's superb."

"No," Phil shouted back. "There is something wrong . . . "

"What do you mean?"

"No, I am not coming."

So I reversed the pitch.

"I don't like it, and I can't do it."

"We'll have a brew, then go for it, okay?"

"No, I don't think I can."

"Just across the next pitch, maybe two, then it's a doddle to the top."

"It's too far. I'm too tired."

"Come on, Lobby, just one more day, just for me . . . "

"Victor, I would have gone down earlier, I've been going for the last four days just for you."

I hugged Phil. What could I say? "Okay, Lob. Let's see

how far we can get down today."

There was no point even considering splitting up, though momentarily I did. We had one rope and one stove. Even if I left the stove with Phil and took a water bottle, I would need to take the rope for the next two pitches. And if I failed to return, it would have been the end for Phil too. He could not have reversed the route to Watts' Dangle without a rope.

We started down at midday on Day 10.

7

We did not reach Base until Day 14. We lost track of time, and there still seems to be a whole day missing. My memories of the long descent are spasmodic. Suddenly the energy, fuelled by optimism, was gone. It was somehow even harder to push the body downhill than it had been pushing up. At one point on the broad shoulder above the sérac barrier we resorted to compass bearings. We had to guess the exact line between the thinly covered crevasses which lay in wait like elephant traps, and we argued bitterly.

"For chrissake, Lob, it can't be down there. Are you trying to kill us both?"

"If you think it's that way you're mad, Victor."

And so on. On this occasion it was Phil who was right.

By late afternoon we had descended as far as the top of the sérac barrier. There we met some Japanese climbers who were based on the Hassanabad side of the mountain. It had taken them two months to fix ropes to the top of the sérac barrier, and they had already fixed 16,500 feet. They told us they had another 3000 feet of rope, and I estimated that this would take them to the top of the Giant Icecream Roll at least. I found their method of climbing somewhat novel, four of them would stand together chatting, while the fifth struggled on his own, trailing the rope for the others. I do not know what they thought of our efforts, they were far too polite to say.

The Japanese made us tea and gave us thin strips of

transparent flesh, which tasted like Bunderfleisch. Phil and I could not agree whether it was more likely to be horse or whale. We were agreed, however, that the green stuff was definitely seaweed. The Japanese fixed rope ran all the way down to their camp on the West Col, just above Watts' Dangle. I remember sliding down their rope, swearing at the descender for snagging at every knot I had to pass.

We reached Watts' Dangle late on the evening of Day 10. We were far too exhausted to make an early start on Day 11. We lay flopped out on the slab, blinking in the morning sun, and trying to remember how to make tea. As we lay there, we could see three spidery figures on the slope below us. They were stopping to rest their heads on the snow at regular intervals, just like some kind of nodding novelty you might buy in a joke shop. As they approached I could see that Mick was wearing two layers of sun glasses, pulled over his glacier goggles. Chris wore John's boot with a green gaiter on one foot and his own boot with a red gaiter on the other side. Boydie had my goat-eaten helmet on, the missing leather straps replaced with bits of green sling, crudely stitched together. Phil and I sat up in our sleeping bags and laughed.

We sat in the morning sun, knowing that we should have been on our way, but unable to move. On the horizon, the skies had cleared for a spell of good weather. Diran and Rakaposhi floated like great white clouds above the valley haze. To their left a nasty steep-looking corner, or pillar, dominated the skyline. Three years later this would be a challenge to take up at closer quarters. Another memory I have of the descent is the hallucinations. I was abseiling past a long granite wall, looking for a crack to place a peg, and convinced myself the subtle discolorations of weathering, and patches of lichen were Egyptian hieroglyphs – vulture-headed gods, and pharaohs in profile did not go away.

I did not mention the hieroglyphs to Phil, and it was

clearly a mistake to have told him about the music. The bivouac that night was particularly miserable. We cut a ledge in soft damp snow and all night long there were small wet-snow avalanches which got inside everything. It was during this night that the music started, the rational part of the subconscious perhaps, trying to make sense of the sound as the wet snow slurried past. I lay back in my wet sleeping bag enjoying the harmony. I listened to Mendelssohn, the concerto with the searching, pleading extrusions from Fritz Kreisler's violin. Was there, perhaps, something almost gypsy there?

"Can you hear the music too, Lobby?"

"Are you joking?"

I dropped the subject, but the music stayed with me for the next three days.

We spent two whole days just abseiling. It was more than we could bear, but there was no alternative. The sting was in the tail, of course. The séracs above the Ring had changed for the worse during the fortnight. We did not want to cope with route-finding as well as everything else. We kept falling asleep, our bodies were like lead. One fit of sleeping took place just before the Dangerous Ravine.

"Come on, Lob, wake up."

"Huh? Oh, oh dear . . . "

"The sooner we cross over, the sooner we reach Base."

"Mumble, mumble . . . the sooner we get down there, the sooner we'll be in the main line of the stonefall."

But I was too tired to wait for twilight. Ominously the music, which had been light and rather baroque till now, began to consist of funeral dirges. Sad choirs sang 'Tallis is dead'. I ignored the warning, and abseiled down into the ravine. The torrent was not so much a stream as a series of connected waterfalls, gushing from the hole in the sérac. Leaving the end of the rope, a skip and a leap were sufficient to reach the half-way boulder. Once there, a glance up was obligatory to check the source for stonefall. To my horror, the sky sported a flock of leaping rocks. I crouched behind the boulder, sitting in the icy water. The rocks crashed and ricocheted past. The air was filled with granite splinters, and a smell like cordite. After five minutes, I took a hurried peep from behind the boulder. All clear. I made an asthmatic lunge, and splashed across the remainder of the torrent to relative safety.

A frightening scene began to unfold before my eyes. Phil was still on the far side. He was crossing under a bluff. Above him the Ring séracs balanced on the smooth slabs. A small stream flowed from under the ice, and made a thin waterfall crossing Phil's path. As he reached this waterfall, it began to dribble rocks. Phil stepped back. The falling rocks grew in size and number. As rucksack-size blocks exploded around him, Phil squeezed himself into a shallow corner under a small overhang, then I saw him creep back up the abseil rope to wait nightfall and a safer crossing.

Back at Base nobody was eating Dai's food. Both Liaquat and Dai, who were not speaking to each other, had attached themselves to John, who Dai insisted on calling Doctor Sahib, and treating him to daily instalments of his hypochondria. John had spent the last two weeks lying down, and was now better, but seeing all this must have inspired Dai's flights of fancy.

After twenty-four hours at Base, I decided to escape. It would be a few days before the A-team returned. Phil, the only one who could stomach Dai's cooking, elected to rest, sleeping in the sun spread out on a borrowed Karri-mat, an inedibly thin open sandwich. John decided to test his back by joining me. We would walk down to Baltit, perhaps cross over to Nagar, take some photographs of Bojohaghur, generally relax and enjoy ourselves. I needed to, the music was still running in my head, but I was back in the world of people, animals, flowers even. The mountain seemed like an alien planet, the kind of reality you

(Above) Conway's view of Conway's Ogre.
(Below left) The magnificent South-West Spur of Latok III above the Japanese Camp.
(Below right) Peering into the crevasse on Latok IV. 120 feet below, Okano was lying on a snow ledge. He had not seen light for eight days.

Above us the ice ramp disappeared, squeezed between two walls of granite. It had taken us into the heart of the East Face of Uzum Brakk.

Looking out from our first bivouac on Uzum Brakk, the (then unclimbed) Ogre II dominates the view on the horizon.

(Above) Phil Butler picking a route through the dirty séracs of the Ring.
(Below) Rimo III, left, and Rimo I.

(Above) Stephen Venables photographed by Dick Renshaw.

(Below left) Under the Capucin.
(Below right) A beautifully sculpted snow roll overhung the ridge on both sides. We bivouacked on the top of the roll.

The Golden Pillar from Melangush Chish.

(Above) From the bivouac above the Slabs we looked out on the Girgindil peaks in the evening light, with the Batura wall and Bojohaghur on the horizon.

(Below) The start of the ice-covered Thousand-Foot Slabs.

The Ice Ear leant out over the Open-Book Corner with no apparent means of support.

(Above) On day 7 the valley fog receded to reveal our descent route, and a panorama, with Momhil Sar and Trivor in the background.

(Below Left) Phil Butler photographed by Mick Fowler.
(Below Right) Mick Fowler.

enter when you read a book, it ends the moment you close the covers. But I was caught in limbo, neither on the mountain, nor back on earth. I wanted to adjust to the new world, so we set off for a damned good meal at Kalb Ali's.

"Tell us, Kalb," John said, wiping a corner of his mouth, "about the musicians we saw today. Are they from here?"

"Yes, they are from Berishal, all music is from Berishal."

"Oh, you mean most musicians live in Berishal?" I asked.

"No, music-making only from Berishal."

"Oh, no music in Baltit, Karimabad?"

"No, only Berishal."

"Why, why only Berishal?"

"Berishals are different, they speak Berishalski. We speak Burushaski. They are forty houses, speaking only Berishalski. Only Berishals make music. Berishal cannot marry Burushaski man or woman. If Berishal man comes to my house, I cannot eat with him."

"You mean the Berishals have the monopoly of music in Hunza?" I said.

"Yes, and also in Nagar."

This was even more bizarre than the mountain world. I began to feel that reality was eluding me.

When John and I returned to Base, the A-team were there. Things had not gone perfectly. They reached a high point at the drafty snow cave, and on the way down Chris had survived a seventy-foot fall while abseiling.

Back in London I was absolutely miserable. A complete failure. Who could I blame for the result of the expedition? Were we wrong to attempt the peak alpine-style? Should we have set up camps at the base of the Three Thousand Foot Slope? Should Phil and I not have gone on from the Col at 19,500 feet? Should we have returned to Base to acclimatise? Should I have left Phil and attempted to solo on? Should we have allowed more time? To this last question, I felt sure the answer was yes. We had been in Pakistan a total of five weeks. Now we were back at our desks. We had had good chances, we wasted them. Somewhere inside, my frustrated soul was boiling in rage. On the surface I was trying to look philosophical and Shiptonesque and believe peak-bagging is vulgar.

It was late when I pushed and squeezed into the Globe. Wednesday night, North London Mountaineering Club night, always crowded. There was Lobby, crushed into the bar. "Pint, Victor?" Somehow Mick had commandeered a table. "Ah, Vic old chap, just the man we were speaking of." "Eh . . . wassat?" I could not hear over the din. Watty and Boydie slouched back, grinning. Lobby pressed the pint into my hand. John emerged from the jungle and pushed a package at me. He leant over and shouted into my ear, "It's from the boys." I opened the package. It was a box of chocolates. On it there was an envelope addressed to "Our Leader". Inside it was a note. It read "Sorry, we did our best."

PART THREE

Rimo, 1985

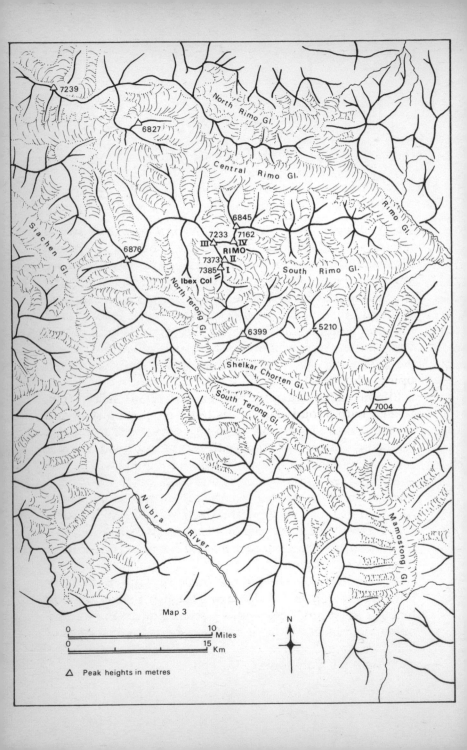

7239

6827

North Rimo Gl.

Central Rimo Gl.

Rimo Gl.

6845

7233 7162

III   IV

RIMO

II

7373

7385 I

Ibex Col

6876

Siachen Gl.

North Terong Gl.

South Rimo Gl.

6399   5210

Shelkar Chorten Gl.

South Terong Gl.

7004

Nubra River

Mamostong Gl.

Map 3

N

0   10
|___|___|___|___|___| Miles
0   15
|___|___|___|___|___|___| Km

△ Peak heights in metres

8

I met Stephen Venables in the Avon Gorge one sunny afternoon in 1979. I was holding the ropes for my friend Simon, while Stephen was also belaying a friend, and we shared a ledge. It was sunny, Stephen had a slightly tousled untidy appearance that put you at ease, and through our casual exchanges we found we had at least one acquaintance in common, a thin giant called Lindsay Griffin. We swapped stories. There were other odd people we both knew, and a promising conversation was developing when Simon fell off.

Simon sailed through the air for about thirty feet, landed with a loud slap on his thigh on a steep slab, and shot out into space once more, to come to a swinging, bouncing, dangling halt slightly above my head. I could see that he was not seriously injured. Simon was not so sure, and his howls of pain and rage must have been audible for miles. It was pure theatre, of course. I lowered him to the stance, and Stephen helped pull him in. After this incident Stephen told his friends that he thought I must be rather cruel because I could not help chuckling at Simon's performance.

A year later, in the dense heat of Raja Bazaar, in Rawalpindi, I heard a distinctly English voice. "Bloody hell, it's Saunders!" Stephen's peeling European face and billowing cricket hat were bobbing above the black sea of heads like a galleon.

"Where are you going?" I asked.

"Kunyang Chish."

"Who with?"

"Dave Wilkinson . . . "

"Oh, the one who climbed with Simon in the Alps last year?"

"Yes, where are you going?"

"Conway's Ogre . . . "

"Who are you going with?"

"Cairns Dixon and Will Tapsfield."

"Is Tapsfield a doctor?"

"Yes, you know him?"

"We were at Oxford together."

I did not hear from Stephen again, until 1st December 1981, when the telephone rang. I had not set foot on a mountain for eighteen months. When I returned from Conway's Ogre, Kathryn, to whom I was married at that time, was five months pregnant. Our son Ben had occupied the space that the mountains would have taken. We moved house, weekends were to be spent at home. My DIY efforts were almost totally ineffectual, because of my allergies. I was constantly wheezing, dribbling at the nose, rubbing ointments into my hands, or changing nappies. I had forgotten that climbing even existed.

"This is Venables . . . "

I had no idea who this man was.

"Stephen Venables, we met in Rawalpindi, remember?"

"Oh yes, how nice to hear from you. How are things with you, did you get up your mountain?"

"No. What I am ringing about is we are going to the Oberland in two weeks' time. It's Dave Wilkinson, Dick Renshaw and me . . . "

"Yes?"

"Do you want to come?"

My mind zipped fondly back to my first encounter with Dave and Dick on my first ever visit to Chamonix in 1978. I was wide-eyed with whatever it is that beginners are wide-eyed about. Dave and Simon had just completed a new route on the Fischerwand. It took them two days, and the entire time was spent under séracs. As they completed the final pitches the band of séracs at the head of the wall collapsed, sweeping their route. Such risks were, till then, completely unknown to me, and yet, in spite of this, Dave seemed to be a sensible and experienced mountaineer, with all kinds of little tricks up his sleeve. When descending unknown slopes he had a way of swaying from side to side to see by parallax the height of potential cliffs hidden by the slope. He tied his mitts to his wrists from the fingertips, so that spindrift would not collect inside them, and so on.

Dave and Simon went back to England. It was late September, the camp sites had emptied. Dick was just about the only other British climber left in Chamonix, except for Billy Ireland. Billy was from Belfast. He fell in love with climbing so completely that he took a job in Chamonix, a *plongeur* in the Hotel Blatière. Billy had also acquired that most prized of Chamonix commodities, a flat. The municipal camping grounds were empty and unwelcoming, and both Dick and I were glad of Billy's invitation. We lolled in easy chairs, drinking the Irish whiskey, with red wine chasers. Loud Irish music. Planxty, or Chieftains . . . can't remember any more. Eyelids sagging. Heads nodding with music or sleep. Slowly we became aware of a dull thunder. Billy looked behind the record player – nothing, in the cupboards – nothing, under the sofa, under the sofa again. Yes the noise was definitely coming from under the sofa. We all got down on hands and knees to listen to the thunder from under the sofa. We turned the music down to listen more closely. Dick, who must have had fewer red wine chasers than the rest of us, understood the meaning of the noise. He sat back on his haunches and announced in sombre tones, "It's someone banging on the ceiling."

"Ah, a broomstick, that'll be it, they are using a broomstick," said Billy with evident satisfaction, as he hauled himself back into his seat, and turned the record player up to the maximum again.

After a little while, and a few more tumblers of whiskey, the thunder began again. This time Billy left the flat. This whiskey, it was Black Bush from Antrim, was really very good I thought, admiring the colour and texture. Dick, who had fallen asleep, woke with a start as Billy burst into the room and flung open the windows.

"Whaa . . . what are you doing?"

"It is the neighbours, they are complaining about the noise, so I am opening the windows to let some of it out."

Dick and I nodded at Billy's inscrutable logic, and drifted back to sleep.

I had not seen Dave or Dick since. It would be great to visit the Oberland with this lot. In fact the weather that year was appalling, the nearest Dave and I got to any mountains was staying three days in the Schmadri Hutte, when Dave tried to teach me the rudiments of calculus, while I told him all I knew about baroque architecture. (Dave got the worse deal.) The one thing that did come out of the fortnight in Switzerland was a conviction that we could at least all get on well together. The chance to prove this came in 1984 when the Alpine Club received a letter from a group purporting to be The Mountaineers of Bombay, offering the chance of an expedition to the Indian Karakoram to attempt the unclimbed 24,230-foot (7385m) peak, Rimo. This was a rare opportunity, as the region had been under disputed ownership since Partition, and access from the Indian side restricted to Indian Army expeditions. Meanwhile the Pakistani government had been selling permits for the peaks in the Siachen area, with access from the west. No doubt an American map showing the Siachen to be in Pakistan was influential. An American expedition made the first winter ski traverse of the Karakoram in 1980 by crossing from Pakistan into the Siachen, up this glacier, down the Baltoro, up the Biafo, and then down the Hispar. In 1984 a Japanese team was given Pakistani permission to climb Rimo, but by now the Indians had caught on, and with the first signs of military intervention the permission for Rimo was rescinded, and the Japanese sent to Bojohaghur, where Phil Butler and I met them on the West Ridge. So now there was an opportunity to climb their mountain.

Stephen, Dave and I jumped at the chance to climb together. Dick was not available but a Cumbrian dentist, Jim Fotheringham, was able to make up the party of four. There were to be six Indians, including our leader, Harish Kapadia, then editor of the *Himalayan Journal*. Harish turned out to be an encyclopaedia of Himalayan knowledge. His team included Meena Agrawal, an orthopaedic consultant working in London, Arun Samant, Dhiren Toolsidas, Xerxes Boga (his brother revels in the name of Chaos Boga), and last on the list was one Muslim Contractor. We had no idea what a Muslim contractor might be till we met him. Muslim was to be the most sensitive and well read person at our Base. But he had the habit of always looking worried, even when making a joke.

Harish was almost rotund. I supposed that the extra weight was his secret weapon – no need to carry food. Harish loved food and cricket. "Forty momoes, not out!" he would declare after a particularly successful innings at the restaurant. In Leh, the capital of Ladakh, he taught us all the different ways of eating mango. They can be eaten green, with salt. They can be spooned from the halved shells. They can be turned inside out and smeared into (and often all around) the mouth. But best of all, says Harish, is the Sensuous Method. You squeeze the ripe fruit till the flesh has become a liquid pulp, then bite off a tiny hole in the skin, through which the pulp is sucked, with lots of noise. We had plenty of time to practise the Sensuous Method, as the expedition was unable to leave Leh for a week.

At first we simply enjoyed the place, visiting temples and stupas. Amazingly, there was also a Moravian church in Leh. The owner of one of the local hotels was a third-generation Ladakhi Christian and he told us how his grandfather, Tashi Tsering, had come to be baptised back in 1905. Tashi was a good Buddhist scholar, but when he read the Testaments brought by the Moravian missionaries he yearned to embrace this new religion instead. The Moravians were housed in the British Compound at this time and therefore trying to keep a low profile, so they refused to baptise him. One night Tashi had a vision of two white-robed figures standing either side of his head and calling him to the Lord Christ. He ran out into the dawn and hammered on the gates of the compound at four o'clock in the morning, bringing the embarrassed Moravian missionary out in his pyjamas. But still they would not baptise him.

This was too much. Tashi abandoned his family, and began to tour Zanskar and Ladakh preaching to the Buddhist and Islamic communities. He had been travelling for six years, when he found himself back in Leh. He saw that his house was empty, his wife remarried and his children living with uncles. Suddenly, he was overcome with remorse. He collected his children, brought back his wife, weeded and planted his fields, repaired his house, and resolved to settle down to sedentary, if proselytising, life. First he converted his family, then, more slowly, a few of his neighbours, helping construct the Moravian church in Leh, and becoming a church elder. Although Tashi's son and grandson were to make journeys as far as Moravia, old Tashi never left Leh again. But today there are about a hundred Christians in Leh.

Mutab Kaolon was another hotel-owner. He came from a family used to providing Ladakh's leading politicians, and his hospitality needed some getting used to. At the Lahrimo Hotel a local brandy was served in half-pint measures, and chased by pints of lager. Waiters kept hovering at the elbow to fill up any half-empty glasses, and soon most of the team were beyond making sensible conversation. Never one to let a consideration like sense get in the way of a good story, Jim told the assembled group a complicated story about the dreaded Croglin Vampire, from what I could make out the ghost of a dentist from Cumbria.

The feast was meant to be a going away party. And the next day we attempted to leave Leh. The truck had been loaded in advance, we would need to leave at 4.00 am, the Khardung La being a one way only road, up in the morning, and down in the afternoon. But our liaison officer had been unable to sort out some minor difficulties. While we were feasting, all the colonels in Leh were also having a party, and could not be contacted by phone. The next attempt took us as far as the outskirts of the town, where a police sentry refused to let us go on. His superior was not to be contacted by phone. Jim thought the phone sets might not be connected to anything at all, and indeed, there were no visible wires. By the time the sentry and Harish had run down to town and back, we had missed the uphill time window. At the third attempt we were informed that our liaison officer had had a heart attack. Again the Army could not be phoned, Meena wanted to see the man, but this was not possible. Much later Harish discovered the man's wife had arrived in Leh that day. "It is not the normal kind of heart attack," he said. We were assigned a new liaison officer, Lt Mahendra Singh. Mahendra soon became Minder.

What we did not know, was that the Indian Army were in the middle of an action while we were trying to reach the battle zone. *The Guardian* reported at the time:

GLACIER BATTLE FLARES

Indian troops beat off an attempt by Pakistani commandos to seize a glacier on the disputed northern border between the two countries and the Pakistanis suffered heavy casualties, Indian newspapers said today.

The Indian Defence Ministry neither confirmed nor denied reports that Indian soldiers repulsed Pakistani infantry and commandos trying to take the Siachen glacier in Kashmir's Nubra Valley.

The Hindu newspaper in Madras said the battle flared on June 8, eleven days after Pakistani forces attempted to capture an Indian border post in the region. It linked the glacier battle to the current US visit of the Indian Prime Minister, Mr Rajiv Ghandi. — Reuter

On the 12th the expedition made its fourth attempt to leave Leh. I can only assume the Army thought that the Siachen war was over for the time being, because we got through the Khardung La without further military hindrance.

Two days of trucking over the Khardung La and through the Nubra valley took us past the Army outposts of Sasoma and Panamik, and eventually up to an enormous encampment by the snout of the Siachen Glacier. We were going to the west side of the Rimo group, mountains we could find no photographs of, other than a very fuzzy image from the east, from de Filippi's 1914 explorations. As far as we knew, our only predecessor was Visser in 1929, yet our valley, the Terong, was easy to find. In 1927 Longstaff advised "Will the party please proceed five miles up the Siachen Glacier, and take the first turning on the right."

The first turning on the right led down to a secondary snout, which blocked the lower end of a five-mile long valley, the upper end being blocked by the snout of the Terong Glacier. A river flowed between the two snouts, disappearing at a mesmeric rate into a hole in the Siachen Glacier. It was a great novelty, this valley of the Two Snouts. Two-thousand-foot granite walls lined both sides, offering some of the finest rock climbing anywhere. Below the walls were beaches of fine white sand, and clumps of conifers and juniper. The wild life was evidenced by the variety of tracks descending to the water. Most of the tracks were cloven-hoofed, suggesting bharal or other forms of mountain sheep and goat, but there were also cats and possibly a bear. The valley was inhabited by katabatic winds, and the fine white dust got into everything, giving our first camp its name, Dust Camp. Sitting around the fire, Harish told us that Terong simply meant 'that valley'. We could imagine the local guides telling Visser, "Oh that? That valley? Yes, we go up that valley."

On the 16th we crossed the Terong river and climbed the glacier snout to look for a Base Camp site. Trying to return to Dust Camp in the dark we had our first experience of the rate at which the river could rise in a day. Our sandy beaches had gone. Trying to cross the river on his own, Jim had been washed downstream, and scrambled ashore very wet and frightened several hundred yards below his intended crossing point, after failing to do an ice-axe brake on the river bed. The rest of us had that arched hole in the Siachen where the river was swallowed by the glacier too firmly in our minds to attempt such folly and Dave and I spent a miserably cold and prickly bivouac on the river bank, insulating ourselves with straw like a pair of Worzel Gummidges.

Two days later the expedition made a camp around a puddle of dark grey clay at a corner of the Terong Glacier. Rocks thrown into the puddle made a delicious plopping noise. Jim and I found that a good size plop would spatter tents twenty yards away. This was Mud Camp. The expedition was short on porters, several had run away when they saw Stephen pop up from behind a boulder dune. He had been wandering around the upper glaciers admiring the views, being at one with nature, and generally proving himself to have a more cultured attitude to the environment than the rest of us. He had several dangling cameras, which the porters thought were binoculars, while his bush hat and dark glasses combined to give him a particularly unsavoury military look. They thought he was spying on them.

Because of the porter shortage, Mud Camp was kept as a supply stage, and team members helped ferry loads up to the Base Camp at 15,000 feet. Harish called the place Lake of Bones, because Visser's party found bleached animal remains here. We found nothing more sinister than raven pellets which when boiled down revealed the bones and bill of a small duck. It was Jim who located the campsite, and to guide the rest of us he built a series of two-legged cairns, which he called Eskimo cairns, at each change of direction. It was quite predictable that Stephen, his mind on loftier things, would walk straight past these and miss Lake of Bones completely. He did, and spent the night out on the glacier, breezing into camp the next day muttering about the delights of sleeping out under the stars without a sleeping bag.

At Base we unpacked the new lightweight two-man single-skin tents. We were keen to see how they performed. Dave was particularly proud of his, which he packed lovingly at the top of his rucksack, ready for our early start the next day. But Stephen was appalled at the sight of the tiny tents.

"I'll never fit in there! They're designed for dwarfs!"

"Oh, I don't know," I said, "they look big enough to me."

"Exactly!"

For his part, Stephen was extremely proud of demonstrating a shiny new pair of crampons that closed on the boot with a scissors motion.

The next morning we made our first Alpine start of the trip. Jim and I would climb together, while Dave and Stephen would pair up for the exploration. The alarm watch beeped at midnight, but I was awake anyway, listening to the groans and gunsharp cracks of the glacier. This was always the worst of climbing, the getting up. My way round it was to get into the sleeping bag fully clothed, and although this always made me feel like a naughty twelve-year-old, getting up to dress in the sub-zero didn't bear thinking about. The surface stream from the Lake of Bones had shrunk, leaving panes of ice, which splintered tinkling under our heavy boots and Stephen's crampons. After an hour tramping across the glacier in the dark, we had to cross another surface stream. Jumping across, Dave fell in and broke his little finger. He was in pain, soaked and, by sunrise, beginning to suffer from exposure.

"I think we had better put up the Dwarf Special," said Stephen.

Dave's pride and joy had no sooner been erected and pegged out than Stephen put his cramponed boot through it. When Dave drew breath in a torrent of abuse, Stephen, sensitive as ever, said, "Oh come on, Dave, you're just being an old woman."

Dave became almost incoherent with rage. "You, you," he spluttered, "well it's not me that's the old woman. It's you! Insisting on wearing your stupid crampons all the time and . . . " and much more in the same vein. Jim and I stood back, and decided to pitch our tent some way off. Back in Lake of Bones for supper that night, Dave amused Harish with cameos of Jim as handsome, me as polite, Dave well-dressed and, longest laugh of all, Stephen as nimble.

9

After Dave broke his finger the weather was unsettled for a few days, allowing him time to recover. During this time we established an Advance Base at 17,000 feet under the West Ridge of Rimo I. The camp was on the Ibex Glacier, leading to the Ibex Col (c 18,000 feet), which was later to provide the route to the East Rimo Glacier. On the fourth day after the accident the clouds left the sky. We spent the next twenty-four hours debating the best line of ascent and waiting a little for the snow to settle. Jim was interested in a steep buttress starting near the Ibex Col, which we referred to as the Crog Spur in honour of Jim and his neighbourhood vampire. In retrospect this is the line we should have chosen. In 1988 an Indo-Japanese team made the first ascent of Rimo I by a couloir system just to the right of the Crog Spur.

Somewhat to the left of this buttress an icefield led up to the West Ridge of Rimo. This was my preferred line. I have always regarded ice climbing as the easy option. Further left again a snow slope led to a col (c 21,000 feet) on the West Ridge. This was Dave's preference. It meant a longer route, as we would have to follow the ridge for over half a mile, before meeting the top of the icefield at c 21,500 feet. There the ridge rose more steeply in a narrow shoulder to the top of the Crog Spur (c 22,500 feet). After that snowfields led more gently up to the summit. Dave's route was the one chosen for our first serious foray onto the mountain and we expected to reach the base of

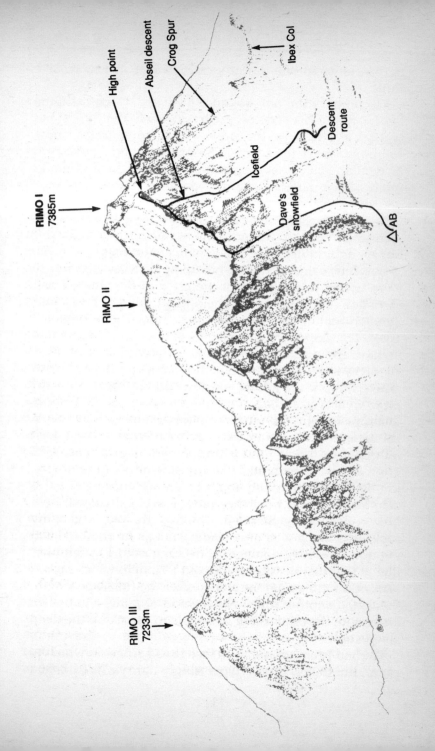

the shoulder in one day from the glacier. It was to take three.

We set out from our Advance Base at 2.00 am, with the lightweight tents. The bergschrund needed a little rope-work, but otherwise the slope was uncomplicated snow climbing. Above the schrund Stephen and I took different lines, with Dave following in Stephen's tracks, and Jim in mine. This annoyed Dave considerably.

"Why don't you two sort yourselves out?" he shouted. "It's a total waste of energy making two sets of tracks."

Stephen began a sentence "Don't be such an old . . ." but thought better of it. Wise man, sometimes.

Dawn was fine, and we were doing well. By 8.00 am we were within four pitches of the crest of the ridge. I had carried a Super 8 cine-camera, and filmed Dave and Stephen trailing ropes up the long slope. Then things fell apart. The slope steepened up to sixty degrees. The snow became armpit-deep, and unconsolidated. The stuff over-lay rocky slabs. Plunging in without style produced horrid skeetering as crampons slipped down rock. Upward movement was exceedingly difficult to sustain. Climbing as a rope of four, the next two pitches took us four hours. We ground to a halt just two pitches below the crest. Last on the rope, I was left waiting for hours at a time, till I grew annoyed, then angry at the slowness of the others. Jim had started fiddling about on an arête trying to exca-vate a rock climb from the snow. Dave, exhausted, held Jim's ropes slackly. Stephen, who had the other end of my rope, was like a well of consideration as he tried to calm me down. Almost apologetic, he suggested I try another line. It was just possible to dig out a trench, which tacked back and forth across the slope. After the first rope length, Steve tied another rope onto the end of mine, and by late afternoon, the other three were able to prusik up the deep steep snow.

We had been hoping for a nice broad ridge on which to camp, but the crest was depressingly narrow. We pitched the Dwarf Specials on the edge of a pair of cornices. Stephen and Dave were cutting a ledge out of the ice, belayed to a single ice screw. Below them on the next cornice down, Jim and I were doing similar work, when a pair of large rucksacks hit Jim on the head. Jim's unintentional interception was fortunate, because the sacks had been clipped into a seventy-foot loop of slack rope, and would have gone at least that far, assuming the one ice screw held. I was not so sure it would have. What was perhaps more frightening was that both Stephen and Dave appeared to be clipped into the same loop. If the screw had failed, the rucksacks, Dave and Stephen would all have gone the distance. In spite of a thorough exploration of the incident, the ensuing argument failed to establish culpability.

Jim and I settled down to brew tea in our two-pint pot, not sure whether to wear helmets against the danger of further rucksack fall, while Stephen and Dave sat up all night boiling an infinite number of brews on their infinitesimally small billy. Where there are two schools of thought, we seemed destined to remain in opposing camps. Long into the night the fierce debate raged between the big billies and the little billies. I was far too tired to take part, and slept uneasily. The next morning, still feeling drained from the snow slope, we made a late start. By eleven o'clock we had only crossed two pitches. The four of us were gathered beneath the next obstacle, a cuboid black tower. The face on our side looked vertical.

"Pointless," announced Dave. "It is 5b at least."

"Oh, I don't know . . . "

Those fatal words. Why can't I resist an argument? I could have gone down the next day with Jim and Dave, instead I found myself at the same spot the next morning with Steve, wondering if Dave and Jim were right, and we were lacking something serious. Sanity for instance. I had hoped that the weather might turn nasty and force us down, but clearly had not hoped nearly enough. The morning was perfect, except for the seven o'clock howitzer salvo courtesy of the Pakistani and Indian armies. I could imagine some innocent snow slope above the Saichen having all hell pounded out of it. At 7.05 am the bombardment stopped, and there would be silence till seven o'clock the next day.

The first pitch was Stephen's. Brittle wintry ice smeared into the back of a wide cleft which split the Black Tower and allowed precarious front-pointing to a group of large spikes. Stephen draped a few slings over the spikes and began to take in the rope. The Black Tower was made of granite. From the belay there was a choice of lines. Directly above, the cleft narrowed into an overhanging chimney, bounded on its right by a repulsive rib of broken rock. Although overhanging, the chimney had several useful-looking flakes, possible hand and footholds, which seemed to adorn the steepest bits. There was also some potential for escaping onto the rib. The alternative was to examine something hidden behind the rib, and hope for easier going. I chose the alternative.

Delicately clambering over Stephen, I looked round the corner, a shallow groove led back to the broken rib. It is not really possible to climb delicately with a twenty-kilo sack, but I tried. The rock was very loose, and there was only one runner, a peg sixty feet above Stephen, which kept pulling out when I tested it, so I pushed the blade back into the crack and left it. Even purely psychological aid can calm the shaking leg, sometimes. I moved up again before finding that I was stuck. The footholds were far apart, forcing my legs into the splits, and the only possibility of a handhold was a brick-shaped projection, which fell off when I rested an axe on it. I watched the brick cartwheel into space, passing between Stephen and his belay ninety feet below. The brick hit the side wall of the cleft, and began to ricochet from side to side, producing explosions of snow, rock and unusual expletives from my partner. The brick left a four inch wide ledge, and as I

116

attempted to mantelshelf onto the ledge I became slowly and unavoidably seized with a constricting fear. The facts taunted like harpies; ninety feet of rope, no safe runners, rock loose, and snowy. My mind felt like an empty vessel. Slowly, as in dream, I tried again to place a crampon on the ledge. Again and again the crampon scraped onto the ledge, then back down, till I was able to convince myself that the move was possible. Standing on the ledge of loose bricks, with infinite stealth my hand reached out to a spike of rock, and pulled. The spike did not move. There were more good spikes above; I shouted with joy, "We've cracked it!"

Four pitches later, in a narrow col between two pinnacles, we hung the Dwarf Special without its poles, happy, anxious, excited. The Pinnacle Col was our third bivouac on the route. There were happy grumbles about space, whose turn to sleep on the crumbling outside edge of the ledge, and we settled down, fully clothed in our sleeping bags, to begin the long process of brewing up. This time it took two hours to brew the chocolate, and finish off the minuscule portions of salami and Smash.

The morning ritual took three hours, and the first pitch of the day was marked, as usual, by those incongruous howitzers. "Good morning!" said the Indian Army. "Good morning!" returned the Pakistani salvo. The hours slipped by, and it was two o'clock, with afternoon sun, collapsing belays, sinking snow, and we had reached the junction of the ridge with the narrow shoulder. Perhaps if we had an early bivouac, we could start the next day fresh, we reasoned. Perhaps we could even climb the entire shoulder in one day. Neither Stephen nor I cared to remind ourselves that we had planned to reach this place in one long day's climbing and it had taken us three.

The Dwarf Special was always crowded with Stephen. The longest dimension was just six feet, and Stephen is six and a bit. Either the bit had to stick out of the door, or Stephen would have to adopt a Z-shape with elbows to park, knees to accommodate. So when Stephen spent an abnormally long time trying to manoeuvre himself out of his sleeping bag, I hardly thought about it. He was just the usual heaving shapeless nuisance. I gave it a cursory kick to protect the brew. But then came petulant howls and the raging at the one-piece fibre-pile suit. The bum-flap had become irretrievably stuck. In his desperation Stephen tore the zip off his suit, and now the bum-flap hung permanently round the back of his knees. I effected temporary repairs by making a rudimentary lacing system, using a Swiss Army knife and the string from the compass. But to go to the loo, Stephen would first have to be unlaced by me, then laced up again afterwards. To my eternal credit, I never took advantage.

The next two days' hard climbing blend together in my mind. I remember Stephen getting the technically hard pitches, bristling with peg runners. I cursed him for not using slings and nuts. But I, by the perversity of chance, inherited the looser, more psychological, leads. Our landmark was a gendarme we called the Capucin, which had until now looked down on us. On the second day it lay below. Switching from one side of the ridge to the other, over and round the tottering pinnacles, we passed from shade to light, then back again. Some pitches had us whooping with joy as we solved the sharp technical problems. These were the good pitches, with ice-filled cracks, small ledges on solid rock, bristling with runners. I can clearly remember one particular section, where for two pitches we followed the centre of a slab of granite which overhung the ridge on both sides. The exposure was magnificent, like space-walking.

At each stop, we surveyed the horizon, the air so clear that the sense of perspective was lost. The mountains seemed within touching distance, and the detail of the valleys beneath like a finely wrought model. Down there at the fork in the glacier was our Base Camp. Those dreadful Travellers' Parathas, that Harish was so proud of, would now be opened, the cook boy would have just made tea, stirring with the 'tea' spoon, a giant wooden spoon used for stirring pots of masala tea. This was no delicate English garden variety, these black tea leaves almost produced a tar and, when stewed with raw brown sugar, full cream dried milk and garam masala, took you straight to heaven. I could taste it from here.

Meanwhile Meena, Xerxes and Minder were climbing up to Ibex Col, and Minder thought he could see us. He shouted at the top of his voice, "Hello! I can see you. Hello!" till Meena could bear it no longer. "Be quiet, or you will bring down the avalanches!" she said, and the trick must have worked. Minder remained silent till they returned to Base.

It would be easy to forget that Base was a whole week's work away, a week in which I could have been drawing elevations, writing specifications, and administering contracts, followed by a weekend climbing gritstone or playing with Ben, with Wednesday evening at the Globe of course. Separated worlds. I began to realise that Stephen was a pretty good mountaineer as the climbing grew harder. He always unveiled that extra ability, just sufficient to get us up the next section, while still apparently on the borders of modest competence. Higher up the ridge, the rock gradually deteriorated.

During one early morning pitch Stephen tried to pendulum into a steep gully past a very loose vertical wall. He hung a sling from a spike in the wall and lowered himself, slowly swinging back and forth to reach the snow in the back of the gully. As he swung forwards, the spike crumbled, and Stephen tumbled twenty feet into the snow. Wearily he dusted himself down, and ploughed a trench up to a snow-plastered corner where he placed a high peg. I dozed while he clipped a sling into the peg, stood up in the sling and placed another peg, then a nut and another peg. Stephen woke me up with his persistent tugging on the rope, the signal it was my turn to leap into the abysmal gully. Because I had been asleep I had not seen him climb the corner, and assumed that he had free climbed it. It was really quite impressive to lead something as hard as this, at 7000 metres, I thought, as I panted up behind, collecting the spare runners. When I congratulated him he had a good laugh at my expense and suggested I needed a new pair of glasses.

The next pitch lay up snow-covered ribs. I felt no apprehension, even though we had already seen snow-covered pitches unmasked as desperately loose unprotected leads. For some reason, we were always ready to be fooled by the gentle lines of the powder. Sixty feet above Stephen the snow reared up to about eighty degrees from the horizontal. Very deep soft snow is peculiar to the Greater Ranges, and Alpine winters. I only once experienced it in the summer Alps, and never in Scotland. Retreating from the Eiger, something of a pastime for me, in February 1979, I watched Stevie Haston flounder down increasingly deep drifts, till his head and rucksack actually passed under a crest of snow, like a surfer buried under the foam. In the summer of '82, with Phil Butler, on the Gletscherhorn (Carrington-Rouse route), the crux was not the steep ice, or rock climbing in crampons, but a vertical snow wall. There were no runners for 150 feet. It was like climbing the side of a haystack for fifteen storeys.

Three years later, I now looked out not on the threatening outlines of the Jungfrau and Eiger but on the vaguely threatening features of the Bilafond peaks, where the howitzers pummelled the opposing armies. I shook my head and remembered. It was a long way down to the last insecure peg. A lot of thrashing about with the axe beneath a small overhang revealed shatter rock, a tottering stack of unbonded brick, which could not take pegs. The powder snow stuck loosely to the wall in defiance of gravity. So how do you climb a loose vertical wall, with two feet of powder snow plastered over it? I don't know. I decided to try a rising traverse by the compaction technique. This is a variation of the Wilkinson Method. You clean a five-foot section of wall, and compact the snow into a soft lump, optimistically thought of as a step. The idea, according to Dave Wilkinson, is for the denser 'step' to spread your load over a wider area of uncompacted snow. Sometimes it works. Mostly you sink through the 'step' and have to start all over again. It took two hours to build a corridor across the brick wall, which culminated in a pinnacle. And on the pinnacle, like the most elaborate coiffure, a beautifully sculpted snow roll overhung the ridge. On both sides.

We bivouacked on the top of the roll. Below, the East Face of Rimo dropped 3500 feet to the Ibex Glacier. Inside the tent the universe was enclosed in slapping green fabric. The stove hissed, producing moist air and noxious fumes, which condensed at the edge of our universe, before being shaken off by the wind onto our damp sleeping bags. We were five days out.

"Prospects?" I passed a bowl of luke-warm mash and a bite of salami to Stephen.

"One day to top of shoulder . . . " Stephen paused to stuff another spoon of mash into his already crowded mouth, "mmmm, then a day to the base of the final slope, then go for the last . . . mmm, burp . . . thousand feet without sacks?"

"Yes," I agreed, taking the empty pan which I half-filled with warm water and muddy chocolate. "Then two, maybe three, days back to the ridge. My God, this chocolate is revolting. Here, you have a drink."

"We have enough gas for five days, and food for three." Stephen slurped the mixture of chocolate and mash. "Actually I quite like it."

"Not much room for error then, eh."

Steve unzipped the tent and poked his head out. "Hey! Look at this."

I squeezed into the entrance. "Crikey!"

We could see eighty, a hundred miles. The wind had

dropped and there was an extraordinary silence. Although it was very cold, we did not feel it because the view was infused with warm glowing colours. After a while I asked Stephen how many visits to the Karakoram he had had.

"Six."

"Have you ever had six days' perfect weather before?"

"No."

"Neither have I. God help us if it changes now." We were miles up in the sky, as we watched the setting sun, silently boiling.

The next day we broke through to easy ground by 4.00 pm. There were no more steep sections of mixed ice and rock to climb. We had nearly reached the top of the shoulder. Before us lay the thousand-foot summit pyramid, before that a hidden col. We had our doubts, of course. At 23,000 feet, who would not? The easy-looking snow might be impossible, there could be giant crevasses spanning the hidden col, the weather might change. We looked up at the dark blue sky, watched the white billows march across the horizon, that distant menace, and yet, in the prevailing winds, we seemed to be in a corridor of clear sky. 4.00 pm was bivouac time. Stephen prodded the snow with his axe.

"It looks flatter up there. I'll go up a pitch and see if we can reach a good spot behind that rock, shall I?"

I nodded, unable to summon the energy to speak. I hoped he would find a site soon. For some reason I had found the day tiring, perhaps it was lack of food, perhaps lack of water. I sat on my rucksack, and watched Stephen climb. Like an ink blot creeping to the corner of the white page, lying on a flat blue table. There was no longer any perspective. Stephen had become a cypher in a two-dimensional picture.

There was a plaintive sound. It was Stephen's voice, faint with distance. "Victor?" How like a buzzard's call it was. I thought of the wet woods under Moel Siabod

122

echoing with the sad Keeooo, as we searched the grey skies for the bird. "Victor?" Stephen called again.

"Whaaaaaat?" I thought I heard him say something about going down again. "Whaaaasat? I caaaaan't heeear youuuuuu."

"We . . . have . . . to . . . go . . . down!" Perhaps he can't find a bivi site, I thought. So I took the rope in. When he got to speaking range he said, "I've dropped my ruck-sack!" It was true. There was nothing on his back. We both peered over the edge. The West Face sloped away and disappeared from the foreground. Beyond that horizon was the glacier, 3500 feet below.

Stephen pointed with his axe. "Do you think we could abseil down there? See if the sack has stopped half-way?"

I could only assume the man was mad with grief, the West Face of Rimo, last time I saw it, looked like the North Face of the Eiger. "What was in your sack?" I asked.

"Tent poles, sleeping bag, camera lenses, food, stove . . . " Stephen looked miserable. "I'd taken it off, and had clipped it into my ice axe. I turned to bring up the rope, when I heard it sliding away . . . there was nothing I could do . . . I am sure that I had clipped it in. I don't understand it."

Jim did. At Base Camp he explained his theory; Stephen was affected by a time warp. All his actions, which would have been the absolutely correct ones for most people, were just out of phase with universal reality. So he had indeed clipped the sack into the ice axe, only by the time he clicked the karabiner shut, time had moved on, and so the krab was clipped onto nothing. Jim was not the only one to use the incident to bolster bizarre theories. Stephen was interviewed by Thames Television when he got home, who asked him if it was not a sign of incompetence to drop the sack. Stephen blinked and replied that on the contrary, it was a test of real competence to do so and still get down in one piece. And anyway, all the greatest mountaineers dropped things all the time.

"Come on, let's get as far down as possible tonight," I said. And Stephen made his way down the trench that we had excavated that afternoon. When it was my turn to follow, there was an enormous loop of slack rope. "Take in!" I shouted. "Take in!" But the rope remained slack. I could not imagine what the matter was. "Take in, Stephen!" No effect. There was a nasty little wall to down-climb, I really did not want to do it on very slack rope but there was no choice. Below the wall, the trench led round a corner, and there was Stephen, the rope round his ankles, jumping up and down, as much as his scissor crampons would let him, and tearing at his hair.

"Why me? Oh, why me?" he howled at the top of his voice.

"Oh come on, Stephen, it was just a rucksack. It could have been you."

"Oh God, I wish it had been me . . . "

"Don't be ridiculous, I need you to get me down alive."

"But I've ruined the climb . . . "

"No you haven't," I said. "You've probably saved our lives. We have got to go down now, and who knows what might have happened to us if we'd stayed on the route another four days. We'd never get off it in bad weather." And the funny thing is, I meant it. I really did not mind the forced retreat at all. In a way I felt relief, we could start going down at last.

10

Without poles, the tent was little more than a nylon bag. It was a miserable night. Poor Stephen was wracked with remorse, and hardly noticed the physical discomfort. He wore my duvet jacket over his legs, and a Gore-tex sleeping bag cover to keep the warm air in. With no food or water, it was an interesting experiment to see how we would perform at 23,000 feet. It did seem as though we were in for a rather rough time. We sat fully clothed, shaking snow and ice in a plastic mug, hoping to melt the powder. The ice did not turn into water. The Indian Army announced the new morning at 7.00 am, their Pakistani co-professionals returned the greeting, and once again we were met by a very clear and extremely cold day. A light breeze sifted the snow round our knees as we began to dismantle the tent. My feet refused to warm up, and after fifteen minutes I could no longer feel any sensation below the ankle.

"I am sorry, Stephen," I said, "we are going to have to put the tent up again, at least until the sun reaches us."

With hardly a nod, he helped me unpack the tent, lay it out on the snow, and crawled into the bag with me. Apart from the fit of anguish, Stephen had not complained once during the climb. He helped me pull off my boots, and while I massaged one foot back to life, Stephen massaged the other. After an hour a luminescence on the tent fabric told us the morning sun had reached us. It was awful for Stephen to see so much good weather. By this time we should have been below the final summit slope. I wondered how long it would take us to get down. Two days? Three? Perhaps we could abseil down the long icefield rather than reverse the ridge. "I think we should go for the icefield," said Stephen, though I had not been aware that I was wondering aloud. When the feet had been warmed up and the tent put away again, we wandered down the ridge a bit and took the risk of following a couloir which we felt probably reached the upper right-hand corner of the icefield. I had seen the feature through binoculars from Base Camp and, though unknown ground, it would certainly be the quickest way out, assuming it worked.

The first abseil into the couloir took us past irreversible overhangs, and looking up from the belay, we knew that we could not climb out if the abseils proved impossible. I began to have bad feelings when, after the next abseil, the rope stuck. We pulled and jumped on the end of it, but always the thing stretched and then snapped back. It would not do to cut the rope, we would need the full length for the next drop.

"This is not good," I said. Stephen looked at me as if I was some kind of pitiful idiot. I suppose it was just a little bit obvious. After a great deal of flicking the rope back and forward and both of us hanging on the end, there was a little trickle of gravel and snow, and slowly the rope began to slide again. Six more abseils took us down onto the icefield. Now we had used up the last of our pegs, but it was all right, there were those long streaks of névé on the ice, where, providing you follow the white bits, you can climb down without difficulty.

By midday I was less than a thousand feet from the glacier. The noon sun reflected from the ice. I felt tired, and had to rest my head on the slope. Stephen, having no sack to carry, was far below. I counted the steps down, front-pointing towards my landmark, a bump in the slope where I promised myself a rest. The counting was

126

supposed to help estimate the time of arrival, it also gave the mind something else to think about other than that hypochondriacal body. Two feet a step. Kick, grunt, fifteen steps a minute. Stab with ice axe, thirty feet a minute. The next bit took several steps while I thought about it . . . and that makes 1800 feet an hour, plus rests of course, that would reduce the figure to 1500 feet an hour. Good. I should reach the glacier in forty-five minutes. Counting steps like sheep, I passed the bump, rest stops becoming frequent. Stephen was 600 feet below, almost on the flat glacier. I was despairingly slow.

Perhaps I could send my rucksack down on its own. In any case, I couldn't carry the thing any longer. I unbuckled the harness. The sack wanted to go, holding it back by the shoulder strap, I shouted to Stephen to get out of the way. But I doubt he could have heard the hoarse croak. I tried again. My voice was hardly more than a whisper now. Too bad. I let the sack go. I only needed one ice tool for the remaining ice, so I had tied the other axe to the sack with a long sling. After the first bounce the axe detached itself, and began to flay the air in a wild gyroscopic dance. The sack leapt in graceful bounds, the mad axe whirling menacingly. Although I had thrown the sack away from Stephen, it soon swerved in his direction and began to track him like a missile, each bounce slightly correcting the aim.

"For God's sake Stephen, get out . . . " but it was no use, he could not possibly have heard. It was fascinating watching the angry rucksack homing in on the man. I could just imagine the Stop press. Famous Mountaineer Axed to Death in Rucksack Revenge Attack. Mr V was mutilated in what is believed to be the first instance of a rucksack turning on a human, it is thought that the act may have been provoked . . . Luckily, the sack overcompensated for direction on its penultimate bound and landed beside him.

The weather remained perfect for another week, during

which time Dave and Jim crossed Ibex Col to attempt Rimo I from the east, while Stephen and I walked up to the North-West Face, and under the great red cliffs of the face we found the battered rucksack was almost empty, the contents scattered over the glacier. The stove was in two parts, a telephoto lens was almost undamaged by the 5000-foot fall. We found several rolls of film, all unused. None of the rolls of the Black Tower, the Overhanging Slab, the Capucin and the rest of the climb could be found. Walking up to the West Face had been a real effort for both of us, and it was clear that we needed to descend to recover.

We heard that the Terong river had risen, and was now uncrossable. It would be a good opportunity for a little active rest. So we took 600 feet of rope to fix a hand-line traverse across the cliffs above the river. After Rimo we felt quite relaxed, perhaps a little too relaxed at times. Once Stephen completed a particularly difficult section of slab climbing to reach a chimney that led up to some ledges.

"We've cracked it now!" he shouted above the roar of the torrent, then promptly fell off, to bob about in the current like a cork on the end of the rope.

Having fixed our thin rope across the polished cliffs above the river, we found a sandy cove, well supplied with driftwood. There were shuffling noises from the shadows as we fell asleep under the stars, and in the morning we found the tracks of a large and presumably curious, cat. The two days we spent alone in that isolated valley remain some of the most enjoyable I can remember.

We returned from the Terong valley to find Dave and Jim had completed a most impressive ascent of Rimo III via the East Rimo Glacier. And now at last, the wonderful weather began to deteriorate. We retreated safely through the sodden Indian Army front lines without being shot at – it was too wet to come out of the canteen – and were fed sweet tea in rum bottles and fried eggs in parathas. We hitched rides with magnificently moustachioed officers and learnt in passing why so many moustaches were still sported in the Indian Army – the moustache allowance of 20 rupees a month had never been done away with since the days of the British. It was a pleasing legacy to pass on.

It was a warm autumn weekend. Stephen and I had driven down to Pembroke with Dick. We had tried to get Dave and Jim down for a reunion. Dick said there was this route he did years back. We went to look for it, walking across the springy grass. Dick could not remember the name, or even where it was. Excalibur? Excelsior? Down by Bullslaughter Bay, said Dick. Bull's Laughter? suggested Stephen. The line we actually climbed was much harder than we bargained for. Too loose and hard for the likes of us. Our exhibition would certainly have made bulls laugh. Afterwards we failed to abseil into a deep cleft called the Gate of Horn, which had foaming breakers smashing around the bottom. The evening light found us grouped round an outdoor table. While Stephen was buying the drinks, Dick asked me if I would climb with Stephen again.

"Of course," I said, "he is one of the best people to be on a mountain with." Dick looked at me for several moments, to see if I was joking.

PART FOUR

Spantik, 1987

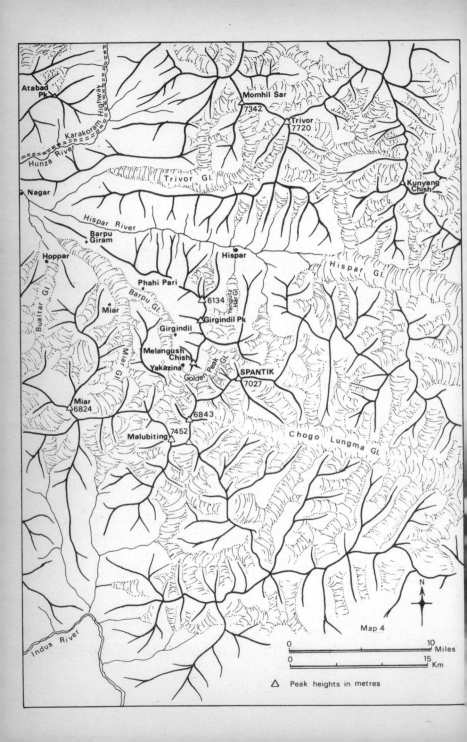

Atabad
Pk

Karakoram Highway

Hunza River

Nagar

Hoppar

Bualtar Gl.

Miar

Miar Gl.

Miar
6824

Momhil Sar
7342

Trivor
7720

Trivor Gl.

Hispar River

Barpu
Giram

Hispar

Phahi Pari

Barpu Gl.

6134

Girgindil Pk

Girgindil

Melangush
Chish

Yakazina

Golden Peak Gl.

Kunyang
Chish

Hispar Gl.

Hispitz Har Gl.

SPANTIK
7027

6843

Malubiting 7452

Chogo Lungma Gl.

N

Map 4

Indus River

0   10
                         Miles
0   15
                         Km

△ Peak heights in metres

11

It was a civil service desk. On the desk there was a tidy file
and a rectangular lunch box, very neat. Carefully arranged, as always, there were the four biscuits and the
two thick-sliced white-bread sandwiches filled with (well
it was Thursday, so it must have been) pâté. On top of the
sandwiches, wrapped in Wednesday's page from the
Radio Times, were two small triangles of fruit cake nestling
against a bright green apple. A space at the end of the box
had been filled with four more chocolate biscuits, not out
of greed, but because the contents would rattle and become dishevelled without the extra packing. Mick Fowler
opened the box with his right hand, pressing the telephone into his ear with the left. He dialled the number of
a local authority architects' department, and began to
cram the pâté sandwich into his mouth.

I had failed to establish any rigour or routine within the
simple confines of my working life. The nearest approxi-
mation were several daily visits to the tea urn on the sixth
floor. Balancing the plastic cup of local authority tea on a
free corner of the desk, I searched for the telephone,
under the usual piles of paper.

Mick: The answer is yes.

Vic: What is the question?

Mick: Spantik . . . I am coming.

And so it was decided. Spantik was, of course, the
23,056-foot (7028 m) mountain we had seen from
Bojohaghur. In 1986 very few had heard of Spantik,

though it had been climbed no less than four times. The peak lies in the heart of the Karakoram, in the ancient mirdom of Nagar, opposite the equally ancient mirdom of Hunza. Although the Karakoram Highway passes no more than twenty miles from it, Spantik is not visible from the road. Yet, from Nagar the mountain is so striking that in 1892 Martin Conway painted it in water colours. It is on the Skardu side of the watershed that the peak is called Spantik. (H. Adams-Carter, the all-knowing editor of the *American Alpine Journal*, says this is a Balti name.) According to some sources it is also known as Yengutz Sar, but this is clearly erroneous, as the peak cannot be seen from the Burushaski-speaking Yengutz Har Valley (Valley of the Torrent of the Flour Mills), and Sar is not Burushaski for peak; it means pond.

The first Westerners to attempt the mountain were the Americans, Fanny Bullock Workman and her husband, Dr William Hunter Workman. In 1906 they climbed the laborious Chogolungma Glacier, taking in the peaks of Chogo and Lungma on the way to the plateau, about a thousand feet below the summit. Their name for the mountain was Pyramid Peak. The Workmans' effort was not bettered till half a century later, when in 1955 a party of West Germans under the leadership of R. Sander made a successful ascent by the Chogolungma Glacier, possibly following the route pioneered by the Workmans. The Germans used the name Spantik but also took it upon themselves to rename the mountain 'Frankfurterberg', one can only hope in honour of their home town. It did not catch on.

Visitors to the region have a habit of adopting bizarre nomenclature. One Italian expedition in 1954 improved on local usage with a Cima Bolognese, though we could not determine exactly which peak this was.

On the north side of the mountain a monolithic pillar catches the evening sun, and gives the peak its Burushaski name, Ganesh Chish, which means Golden

Peak. This was the nasty thing on the horizon that we had seen from Bojohaghur – the Golden Pillar. The Golden Pillar is marble, the rock crystalline, almost sugary in parts, but often sound. The Pillar is the coup de grâce of a vertical outcrop of this metamorphic limestone, which leapfrogs the glaciers from above the village of Nagar. Looking out from high on the Golden Pillar, we would be able to see the cream-yellow rock, arking from glacier to glacier like a series of rainbows.

Further enquiries revealed a little of the mountain's history. From Poland the encyclopaedic Zbigniew Kowalewski sent us some photographs taken from Kunyang Chish. Nazir Sabir, Doug Scott and Tadeusz Piotrowski (who perished on K2 during the tragic summer of 1986) each kindly donated 'front on' prints, which all but persuaded us to cancel. The Pillar was clearly enormous, perhaps 7000 feet from glacier to top, and also clearly very steep. There were menacing looking séracs along its top edge. If we could not climb Bojohaghur, surely we had no business on this thing. Two factors kept alive our enthusiasm for the project. First of all, we were firmly assured that the Pillar was made of perfect granite. So much for geologists. Second, from the safety of the Globe, and well filled pint glasses, all things always seemed possible.

"It's no harder than the Walker, just look at the angle on this photograph . . . "

"'Nother pint, Victor?"

A team coagulated among our drinking companions in the Globe. It was to consist of the Bojohaghurites Phil Butler, Mick Fowler, John English, and myself, together with two NLMC members new to this sort of thing, Liz Allen, John's fiancée, and Bruce Craig, a New Zealander who was my regular rock-climbing partner at the time. Bruce worked for a firm that installed mechanical ventilation systems. His part of the job involved the air-conditioning ducts so, when asked, he described himself as a duct erector. Say duct erector with a strong NZ accent and it comes out as duck director which can cause some confusion. As on Bojo, George, Mick's father, would join us at Base Camp.

A very large number of things went wrong from the start. All the Himalayan countries charge a fee which entitles an expedition to attempt a named peak. Spantik cost us £720. The last date for submission of applications to the Embassy of Pakistan was 30th October 1986. As a result of administrative dysfunction, three British expeditions were prevented from paying their peak fees even though the completed application forms were accepted by the Embassy before the deadline. The Embassy staff, in London, insisted that our money would be only accepted when we received permission. Islamabad took the opposite view. And worse, not only would our applications not be 'entertained' without the cash, but since we had failed to deposit the money by the due date, our applications were automatically refused. One of the three expeditions, Duncan Tunstall's to the Ogre, turned their attentions elsewhere. Roger Payne and Julie-Ann Clyma, applying for the Gasherbrums, embarked on a campaign of letter writing, and so did we.

In January an official letter of permission was received by Duncan Tunstall for the Ogre. I can only assume that this was because, since changing his plans, he had not made a nuisance of himself. In a fit of inspiration, July and Roger decided to marry each other, and invited His Excellency, the Ambassador for Pakistan, to the wedding. His Excellency replied by return, that though he was unfortunately not able to attend the reception, he was glad to confirm their permission for the Gasherbrums. The Pakistan government decided at the same time to allow our application, saving the Spantik team from any necessary marriages . . . phew.

July in Rawalpindi is like a circotherm oven, the kind with a fan to make sure you brown all over. Phil Butler and I flew out a week ahead of the others and booked into the pricey Flashman's Hotel. Mrs Davies' Hotel, where we had stayed in 1980 and 1984, had been flattened, razed by a property speculator, who did not have enough cash to develop the site after all. Marijuana grew where the expedition rooms used to be. The decaying Raj dining room was reduced to the rubble of its foundations. The beautiful shade-giving trees and lawns had been grubbed up, the place was a scrubby desert.

Phil and I spent the days dealing with the Ministry of Tourism, buying food, and organising transport. We spent a lot of time in the various bazaars, each one a ghetto for a particular product. All barbers were on one street, near the stove market. Food and tarpaulins could be bought in Raja Bazaar. In the crowded alleys I glimpsed a boy trotting on all fours. He cannot have been more than ten years old, with a pretty face, impish and bright, but probably crippled as a baby to give him a living as a beggar. Gestures and half understood directions led us in the midday sun across the river bridge to the Kashmiri Bazaar. Our goal was a bus company based near the 'Nerwalty Senemar'.

Here and there a doorway, cornice or window caught my attention. I remember a verandah protruding from the terracotta-washed building, the little balcony was of clear Neo-Palladian inspiration, a stone ballustrade, a pair of Corinthian columns, a fine deep frieze and architrave, small urns with exquisitely worked micro-columns and domes to shade the trailing plants. The entire upper storey consisted of bays with ogee arches and delicate stone screens perforated with diamond-shaped holes. The screens filled the arches, giving shade and cool to the rooms behind.

We crossed the river which cut a great ravine through the city's red clay and was lined with green terraces. A buffalo wallowed lazily under the burning sun. The eyes saw all this, but the nostrils registered the river's true nature, a rich organic soup, ripe to start life all over gain. There were a number of horse-drawn wagons and taxis and, slowly but perceptibly, my breathing became laboured. Rotten fruit and pulp lined the street, a cartload of scrawny chickens in baskets clucked and fidgeted unshaded from the merciless sun. I could hardly breathe as I watched the birds ride towards the nearest restaurant. I had forgotten to bring my Ventolin inhaler.

It is rather important in Rawalpindi to ask questions in the form, "Which way is . . . " rather than "Is this the way to . . . " It took us two hours to find the Nerwalty Senemar. When we arrived, we could see it was the local picture house, the Novelty Cinema. By now I was having a major attack of asthma, and needed to get back to my inhaler. We grabbed the nearest taxi. Ventolin is wonderful stuff. One minute you think you are dying. One puff, and next minute there is ecstatic relaxation. After the Nerwalty episode, Phil and I retired to the hotel's tiny swimming pool. Swimming was the only form of exercise possible in Rawalpindi.

On the third day I returned to our room after swimming to find a strange rucksack by the door and the following conversation wafting out into the passage.

"No, Craig. Bruce Graham Craig. That's right. I'm a duct erector . . . no, not a duck director . . . I erect ducts . . . "

Bruce had arrived from New Zealand with a wild punk haircut and several earrings.

Over supper we prepared the expedition food list, on the back of a hotel envelope, using our version of the Shipton formula – one kilo per man per day: roughly one third rice, flour and sugar, one third pulses and vegetables and one third fats, such as ghee and milk powder. Actually Mick had prepared a meticulous food list, based on a complete schedule of all the meals each member would eat, but I had forgotten to bring it from England. It made me feel guilty to think of all those hours Mick had spent at his civil service desk, ruling lines, filling squares marked Breakfast: Team 1: Choice A, B, C. The guilt did not last long enough to cause any noticeable discomfort and I swore Bruce and Phil to secrecy.

The team was congregating. After Bruce, our appointed liaison officer turned up at the hotel. He was a civilian physician from a family of physicians. Dr Iqbal Mohammed Ahmed took us by surprise.

"So you are all from the North London Mountaineering Club? I have received very good reports about the club."

Iqbal knew all about us. Strangely, that did not stop him joining the team. Iqbal was a bibliophile, with a prodigious memory, and a member of the Pakistan Alpine Club. He was very keen to help, and took me to a military food exchange, where 'authorised personnel' could buy tins of tuna and cheese at much reduced rates. While Iqbal dealt with the bureaucracy, I watched an old man sweeping the yard. There was something familiar about the switch, it was a green-leafed branch, no not a branch, more of a bush. I took a closer look at the nettle-like fronds. The old man was sweeping the yard with cannabis! I pointed this out to Iqbal, who said, "Yes, they are just the right shape, aren't they?"

After Iqbal we had news from George, who was trekking with Karakoram Experience. We would pick him up in Gilgit. Mick, John and Liz were due to arrive the next day, and we had arranged a Ford Transit from Sargan Services, (Nerwalty Branch) to pick us up after they arrived. Meanwhile familiar faces passed by. Nazir Sabir, the Pakistani mountaineer, whom I had met in 1980 and again in 1984, visited us. He had married a Japanese woman who had been trekking with the Japanese team Phil and I met on Bojohaghur. Nazir beamed happily as he announced his departure for Japan, his wife was expecting their first child.

Next Duncan Tunstall arrived with Phil Bartlet. They were going to Snow Lake with Stephen Venables, whom they had lost somewhere in Raja Bazaar. They left us packing, labelling and itemising sack contents. Stephen arrived shortly after they left.

"Hey, Victor, have you seen Duncan or Phil? I think they've got themselves lost in the bazaar. Have you had dinner? Let's eat out at the Silver Grill, I'll treat you. Oh by the way, are you going to Gilgit? Good. Then could you be really kind and leave this bag at the Hunza Inn for me?"

I am told there is no such thing in nature as a free lunch either.

This time we drove to Gilgit overnight. It is far less frightening, you can't see the precipices. There we picked up George, the rice and kerosene. Not forgetting Stephen's rucksack, we drove out towards Hunza. This is the exciting part of the Karakoram Highway, so I travelled the distance with my eyes shut tight.

We were into Burushaski-speaking territory again. The last Englishman to speak fluent Burushaski was, as far as I could tell, D. L. Lorimer, political agent in Gilgit during the 1930s. Lorimer had actually written the first, and possibly only, Burushaski grammar. I had spent countless lunch hours looking for his publications in England. Neither the School of Oriental and African Studies, nor the British Library had anything on Burushaski, but I eventually tracked down a dusty and faded copy of his wife's book in the Library of the old India Office. It was called *Language Hunting in the Karakoram*. Emily Lorimer had little to say on the origins of the language, except that there appeared to be no known relationship with any other language. Dumaki, on the other hand, the language of the musicians, that tribe-within-a-tribe, has been tentatively identified by her husband as belonging to the same group as gypsy Romany.

The Karakoram Highway crosses from the right bank (Hunza) to the left bank (Nagar) of the Hunza river at the village of Ganesh. The bridge was built by the Chinese with Chinese dragons for decoration, crudely applied blobs of red paint enhancing their leering mouths. It was at Ganesh that we exchanged the discomfort and fear of the Transit for the sheer terror of four overloaded jeeps. Our road left the highway to become a rough dusty track with terrible cliffs, and crumbling verges. Sand dunes crossed the track at intervals. There was a very old suspension bridge, which made a fair imitation of the Tacoma Narrows bridge snake dance when the top-heavy jeeps wobbled up onto the rotting timber sleepers. I leapt out of my jeep to walk across the lively, undulating platform with Mick and tried hard to concentrate on something else. I was still thinking about the musicians. I said to Mick, "The problem with Dumaki history is that Lorimer says they originally came from Baltistan . . . See?"

"What *are* you on about?"

"Well, it's obvious, isn't it? I mean, Balti is a Tibetan dialect, and Dumaki is Indo-Aryan, so if they came from Baltistan, where did they come from before that?"

"Victor, what's that got to do with getting the jeeps up to Nagar?"

After the suspension bridge our road took us past Nagar, where we stopped to inform the Assistant Commissioner of our presence. The jeeps bounced and slid to a halt under a parade of poplars fed by a pearly, mica-laden Go-Tsil. A footpath led us up a steep grove of ancient apricot trees, and then to a sagging boarded door in a white-washed stone wall. We passed into the walled garden, where the AC's house appeared to be floating among clouds of flowers. Behind the house a sharp fang of rock menaced the distant horizon. I gasped. It was our first sight of the Golden Pillar.

"Hey, hey, Mick, look! That's it . . . that is it!" It looked so enormous and so steep, I began to feel the need to go home. Mick and Iqbal turned to see what the terror was all about.

"Apparently that's what we've come here to climb," said Mick. "Apparently we enjoy being frightened on steep little bits of rock." Mick's 'apparent' nonchalance made my stomach feel even weaker. Tentacles of apprehension crept over my bowels.

The AC was the Mir of Nagar's cousin, and a sportsman, so he opened the conversation with the English batting performance. "Such a pity, what a collapse! It is really hard for us to support England, when they simply insist on losing all the time."

"Yes, I suppose we're going through a rough patch," I said trying to avert my eyes from the horizon. I had to stop thinking about that monstrous Pillar or I would never get there.

Tea arrived with apricots, the talk turned to local customs, free-style polo, and bharal hunting, poetry, Lorimer (the AC remembered the man), the garden, (several of the AC's trailing plants had European origins), and eventually to our choice of cook. After our disaster on Bojohaghur, we resolved to hire a proper cook for Spantik. We had begun the search in Rawalpindi. One name kept cropping up, that of Rajab Zawar of Nagar. The AC sent an attendant to find him.

"Rajab will meet you at the Hoppar Rest House," he told us, adding, "You know Zawar, in our language, means pilgrim?"

"Oh, like Haji?"

"Indeed, he has made the pilgrimage to Mecca."

Rajab stood on the Rest House steps, his large broken and yellow teeth displayed in a friendly smile. He looked straight at us, as if posing for a camera. He was barely four foot tall. We liked him. As the swirling clouds of brown dust began to settle around the jeeps, it emerged that not only Rajab, but every able-bodied man and boy, from miles around, was in attendance, looking for work. I cannot get used to the efficiency of the Karakoram grapevine. Perhaps there is telepathy after all.

Hoppar is the name given to a clutch of five hamlets grouped half an hour's drive above Nagar, on the edge of the Bualtar Glacier. The Hoppar Rest House is, in fact, in the hamlet of Hoshal and commands a fine view of Nagar, with Bojohaghur as the backdrop. (Thankfully it was not possible to glimpse Spantik from Hoppar.) There was no plumbing in the washrooms, so it was most important to fill the bucket from the nearby Go-Tsil before using the loo. Unfortunately, the Go-Tsil was stoutly defended by prickly thorn bushes. Because of these complications, George decided to visit his morning ablutions on the local countryside. When he returned he complained at length about the crowds of prospective porters following him everywhere.

"I walked miles over there, just getting ready behind a wall, when this bloke pops up and offers me his credentials. Been up Malubiting, and all sorts."

"And did you show him *your* credentials, George?" asked Bruce.

This provoked the expected loud guffaws. Sometimes it was hard to credit that we were a team of thirty-year-olds. Twelve was, perhaps, the average mental age of the expedition.

We rested at Hoppar for two days. The first day was spent packing and weighing porterloads, Liz and Phil doing all the work, while Mick and Bruce explored a route across the Bualtar Glacier to the ruined hamlet of Shiskin whose water supply had dried up in the 1970s. This exploration was necessary because the Bualtar was surging at twenty-four feet a day, and any paths on the ice had to trace a route through a complex maze, which changed every few hours. The Hoppar men told us it would take three days to cross to the far side, a distance of about a mile and a quarter. At that rate it would take nine days to reach our Base. A quick calculation on the back of a Flashman's envelope showed that we simply did not have enough money to pay the men for more than six days' walking. Mick and Bruce probably saved the expedition.

Contracting the porters resembled an extended game of chess. The main participants sat on the verandah, as if on stage, the crowds milling below asking for progress reports, and occasionally passing up trays of tea. In the opening phase it was established that all the porters would be hired from Hoppar. They would be drawn from each hamlet according to the number of households.

The men were represented by a contractor, a Hoppar councillor, who explained, "It is because Nagar take all expeditions to Rakaposhi and Diran, and Hispar men take expeditions to Hispar side, with Nagar help. So it is traditional for Hoppar men to take Barpu expeditions."

They concede us a Nagar cook, but what would we concede them in return? It was a trap of course, there was no concession there. The contractor thought it would take seven or eight days to reach Base, so I produced maps, Iqbal the Government regulations, which required the men to walk ten kilometres per day. I thought it should take three or four days. We argued at length, until we compromised at five days. The local policeman and the tesildar (government official) stood on the verandah to deter foul play. After two hours we agreed a set of day stages. The middle games continued with wage agreements, then food allowances, sums in lieu of glacier boots and sunglasses, and suddenly we were into the end game. This phase drew on into the night, as John examined each candidate, and I took their signatures or thumb prints. One man of seventy said he was thirty-five, another was impersonating his brother. As all of them were called Mohamed, and or Ali, it was all rather confusing and time consuming.

It took us five days to walk to Base, we crossed two glaciers, the Bualtar and the Barpu, on the first day. Thereafter, we followed a delightful ablation valley to the flea-ridden goat-herders' settlement of Barpu Giram, where Phil, Bruce and I became horribly infested.

"There is an ancient Arab curse," said Phil.

"What's that?"

"May your left ear wither and fall into your right pocket; and may your armpits be infested by the fleas of a thousand camels."

An easy day's walk took us to Phahi Pari where a team of Canadian geologists were encamped for the summer.

"Hi, I'm Marty. I'm a sort of resource manager for this expedition." Marty and his colleague, Paul, produced photographs of the base of the Golden Pillar. They were glossy black and white prints, a big black cliff rose straight out of the glacier and into the sky. Those nasty tentacles were starting all over again.

While we examined the photographs minutely, our sirdar, Ibrahim, was showing Iqbal his hunting rifle. It rather worried us that our porters chose to bring guns with them. Two German trekkers were said to have been murdered by Nagar men not many years earlier. But this was ibex country, and these slopes were traditionally visited by the Mir who, between bouts of free-style polo and hopeless cricket, found time to chase the elusive creatures. Ibrahim used to peer through his binoculars at specks which I could not even imagine, and explained the main difficulty in ibex hunting.

"I creep up very quickly, but when they see me they run away. The ibex are very sensible."

The next night at Girgindil, at 13,000 feet, it snowed all night long. I asked Ibrahim how the men felt about crossing onto the glacier while it was snowing . . . we could only afford to pay them one rest day.

"The problem is the weather, this is nonsense weather."

We decided to wait till midday before moving. Meanwhile I talked to Ibrahim about Burushaski, and discovered the language has four genders, male, female, animate and inanimate.

"Which one are you, Vic?" shouted Mick.

"As none of us has had breakfast yet," Phil answered, "we must all be the fourth gender."

145

After breakfast, when we graduated from the fourth gender, the clouds lifted enough for the expedition to get under way once again. The porters were walking ever shorter day stages, which they said were the traditional stages handed down by their grandfathers. Day 5 ended at a place called Yakazina, the Bear's Lair. The men would go no further. Yakazina was barely two and a half hours' walk from the last stage. There was no natural water supply. Although there were fine views towards Malubiting, Spantik was not visible.

"This is very disappointing," I said to Ibrahim. "Let's go round that spur and see if there's a better place."

Thirty minutes later we reached a flat paddock with a full running stream. It was south facing, and pointing up the valley into the clouds, Ibrahim said, "Ganesh Chish."

"This is where we want the camp," I said.

On the trot back I rehearsed a little speech for the porters, while Ibrahim, who had left his rifle at Yakazina, kept sadly pointing at sitting partridges. We were back at Yakazina within the hour. I explained what we wanted to Iqbal, who explained to the porters. It was obviously a disadvantage to speak fluent Urdu, because he was immediately drawn into bitter arguments with the men, who then began to argue amongst themselves, one hamlet against another. After half an hour of this furious democracy Ibrahim walked over to our group, shaking his head, and spoke first to Iqbal (always a bad sign). Iqbal turned to us.

"It's their traditional stops. Arranged by their grandfathers to give the descendants a good living. They could go three more hours for you, but when they get back to the villages the others will criticise them."

"Let me have a word with them direct," I said.

"No, I don't think you should," said Iqbal.

"You'll make it worse," said John and Mick.

"But we have nothing to lose," I said as I walked over to the group of porters. I stood on a boulder to increase my

146

presence and spoke through Ibrahim.

"We have been straight with you . . . " Ibrahim translated into Burushaski, and a few heads nodded. "We bought you a goat, and yesterday you only walked one and a half hours. We do not complain. We would like you to walk just one hour more. You are strong and I am weak, but it took me thirty minutes. If you want to stop here, I will thank you. If you go on with me, I will also thank you."

I continued standing on the boulder to try and hypnotise the men. Iqbal appeared at my side and began saying, "It's the same thing, they won't change the traditional . . . " Then an old porter called Gulam Mehedi came forward. He was a giant, bald as a vulture, with wrinkles from forehead to neck, but a gentle gap-toothed giant, who appeared to be spokesman.

"You are good," he said, "and for you we will give one hour more."

But first they had tea. And so we reached our Base Camp at 12.30 pm on 14th July, 1987.

12

Gulam Mehedi led the porters in the usual bear-hug leaving ceremony, as the men flung their arms around each one of us in turn, except Liz, who sat on a mound watching. It's an Islamic country.

"Come and join in, Liz," Bruce shouted.

"And catch all those fleas?" replied Liz.

I felt rather lonely as our thirty porters left in single file. Liz said, "Right, let's get on with it. Victor, you're in charge, where do you want the tents."

Leaving Liz to organise the tents, Phil, Iqbal and I decided to build a kitchen for little Rajab Zawar, but we had the wrong end of the stick. Within minutes Rajab had made it clear that he did not want our interference, unless it was to help transport rocks to the kitchen building site. Although Rajab was tiny, he was immensely powerful, because it took three of us to lift the chosen boulders onto his back. I watched fascinated as the kitchen grew over the next two days, built against a large glacial erratic, which served as one side. The remaining sides had shelves and storage holes built in as the walls were raised to a height of four feet, the height at which Rajab could stand up straight, once the tarpaulin was draped over the walls. Special spaces were allocated for the Tilley lamp and flat stones laid to pave the floor. By the end of the second day, all eight of us were sitting round the kitchen, watching Rajab completing his great work.

He indicated where he wanted the food stored: sacks of

rice and flour to sit on; potatoes and some pretty indistinguishable greens, not to sit on; boxes of tins that could be sat on, but at some cost to the backside; hessian bags of limes, apricots, garlic heads, onions and fresh chillies (fatal if sat on) were neatly stacked where Rajab could easily reach them. Spices, cutlery, crockery, everything had its predestined home, and only Rajab knew where that was.

Meanwhile we had unpacked our own equipment and prepared for our first acclimatising efforts. Mick, Iqbal and I left at 9.00 am the next day to climb Melangush Chish (Cima Bolzano in Italian), with the idea of surveying the approaches to the Golden Pillar. Melangush was just under 17,400 feet and Base was 13,000 feet.

After eight hours of painful slogging through deep snow, and scrambling over loosely accreted ridges, of headaches, eye pain and general glacier lassitude, we found ourselves staggering about on this very minor summit, wreathed in thin clouds. Mick and I complained about our symptoms, Iqbal had gone unusually silent. After a few minutes, Mick said, "Ah Victor, old friend, I believe congratulations are in order."

"Eh?" Why was the man holding out his hand at me?

"Your first Himalayan summit!"

There was no convenient cliff I could push him off.

We thought that it would be a good idea to bivouac at 16,400 feet at the Col below the summit. But the altitude was getting to us. Mick's eyes hurt so much that he had to erect our tent with them shut tight, and made a brew of something called Sip, which we had bought in Raja Bazaar. It was very diluted, but Iqbal said it would taste even worse if concentrated. By 6.00 pm the clouds had dispersed, it was a beautiful evening. We had brought up several cameras, including a Polaroid, with the intention of using the prints as a guide once on the route. This experiment failed miserably because the detail was far too small, and because the chemical oozing from the blotchy prints made me hesitant about sticking them down my front, wondering what sort of holes the corrosives would develop in my shirts, or me. I also took lots of photographs of Mick, jutting out his chin, decked out in every stitch of Berghaus clothing we had, leaning his maligned Cyclops rucksack against his Yeti gaiters, the Golden Pillar glowing gold in the background. Berghaus never did use any of those.

The next morning we did not bother with breakfast, we felt too ill. Thundrous headaches and no little pills. We had intended to continue from the col to ascend the feature we called the Pap of Girgindil, instead we tried out our light-weight radio to let Rajab know we were coming down. There was a lot of crackle, but no answer.

Three hours later, we had all taken tea and Anadin at Base. John, Liz, Phil and Bruce had set off for Melangush early in the morning, and would be back the same night. Rajab beamed his yellow smile and produced a bowl of steaming water for Mick and me to wash our hair, which was fine for the soapy bit, but rinsing had to be done in the stream. The ice cold water was like a Chinese vice.

Iqbal said, "Was that you screaming?" Later he washed his entire body in the stream . . . yecht!

When the others returned from Melangush Chish, Bruce disappeared into his tent, because of sunburn, he said. Phil complained he had waited on the col all day, tripod and camera at hand, for the sky to clear. Iqbal slumbered in his tent, and George pottered about, undecided whether to wear his false tooth or not.

Mick was glued to the binoculars. We estimated our headwall to be about 4000 vertical feet. Mick was giving out the route description.

"And now the steep groove that I cannot see, but I know it's there, because I saw it last night from the col, and there's a particularly hard pitch for Victor, up behind the Chandelle . . . don't interrupt me now, I haven't finished the climb . . . Right?"

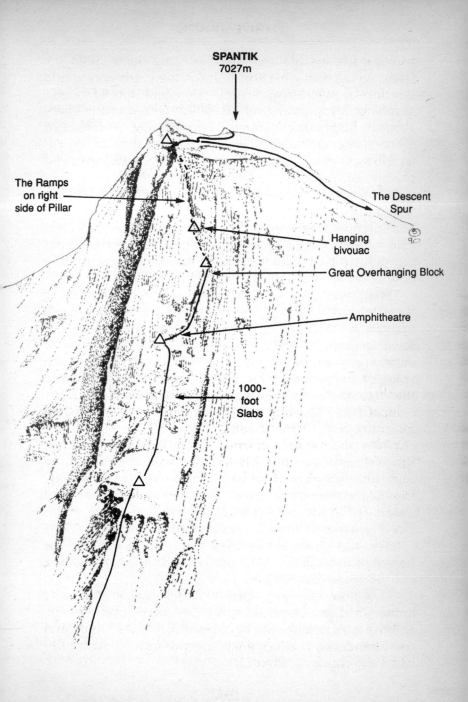

SPANTIK
7027m

The Ramps on right side of Pillar

The Descent Spur

Hanging bivouac

Great Overhanging Block

Amphitheatre

1000-foot Slabs

Mick lowered the binoculars, "I've finished the climb now. We can all go home."

About two hours up the moraine, there was a tall cairn, marking the site of the camp used by the Canadian glaciologist, Professor Hewitt, directly across the small Golden Peak Glacier from the Pillar.

Mick, Bruce, Phil and I spent the night of the 17th at Hewitt's Camp returning to Base for breakfast. We brought binoculars and note pads. The route was in four parts, not including the descent. The first part was the First Tower, rising straight out of the glacier for 1300 feet. Next a serpentine snow arête led to a pocket handkerchief glacier which we called the Hangengletscher. The third part was the point of the exercise, the Headwall, which looked impossibly steep, and finally, from the apex of the Golden Pillar, there would be some two miles of summit slopes before reaching the top. It would not be desirable, perhaps not even possible, to descend the Pillar. But a convenient snowy spur, which landed in the Golden Peak Glacier not far from Base, looked like our best chance of getting off the mountain. Should we ever get that far.

During the next evening, we packed our rucksacks for the first close inspection of the route, but it was sleeting, so we spent our first truly miserable morning at Base, and I spent the morning complaining about the tent.

"I simply can not believe the designer has ever camped out in the rain . . . it is quite incredible . . . for a base camp tent . . . there is no weatherproof area by the entrance for boots and wet clothing . . . this tent needs a bell end . . . how on earth are we supposed to keep the mud off our sleeping bags?"

"Leave 'em outside," said Mick.

"Oh yeh, and have wet boots whenever it rains?"

Meanwhile George and Liz had found some canvas porter bags, which they cut up and stitched to the kitchen tarpaulin, constructing a weatherproof entrance. Phil and Bruce were still packing and sorting their climbing sacks, and the two doctors spent the morning asleep.

Inside the kitchen, Rajab had been at work. He made chips fried in ghee for lunch. The dish was ringed with onion slices, runner beans, cabbage, and sliced hard boiled eggs. A dressing of lime juice, garlic and slivers of green chilli had been drizzled over the yellow mound. Side dishes of dhal, again with lime, and a huge pot of basmati rice supported the main dish. Rajab explained that he had worked as a cook in Gilgit, at a celebrated eating house called the Tourist Cottage. I remembered having made a special visit to the place in 1984, and yes, Rajab said he had been there at the time.

After lunch the weather improved a little, and Mick said, "Apparently it is time to go and frighten ourselves on steep little bits of rock, again."

We hoisted our twenty-eight-kilo rucksacks onto each other's backs, and staggered off towards the moraine. Iqbal looked a shade wistful at being left out of the climbing, but said he would bring a spare rope up to Hewitt's with George. Within minutes of leaving the camp, Mick was complaining about his rucksack.

"What this sack needs, is a good pair of side pockets . . . and no straps."

Then it began to sleet again. The Headwall looked as if it could be reached by straightforward, but long and serious, climbing. The Snow Arête was flanked by large cliffs on both sides. It was rather like the roof of a hillside terrace. As long as you stayed on the ridge, you would come to no harm. The First Tower supported the lower end of the terrace roof, and the Tower, in turn, was split by a narrow ice gulley at the top, which fanned out easily onto the glacier below. It took us an hour to cross the glacier, roped together, the only sound the clink of crampons over the crunching snow-ice and occasional exchanges.

"This way round this crevasse?"

"But remember to curve right again afterwards."

"Keep an eye on this hole here." And so on.

A frisson of expectation ran through my finger tips as I untied the rope below the Tower. Sack down, spread out the contents. Crunchy bar into mouth, helmet onto head, ice axes untie from sack, swing sack back onto shoulders. Shivering with cold, and anticipation, as Mick soloed up in front, while I trailed 300 feet of rope.

"Why don't you put it in your sack, Vic?"

"It makes the sack lighter." We always had this argument.

"But you've got all that extra friction."

"I know, but it seems to work, and the weight comes onto your waist, not the back. Also the rope is ready and out in case we need to tie on."

Sunrise met us at the top of the Tower at 7.30 am. By 8.30 we had retreated from the rapidly softening Snow Arête, and decided to wait out the day on top of the Tower. Mick spent the morning making extra ventilation holes in his gas stove, with his ice axe. He probably doubled the ventilation, but it still smelled of unburned fuel and we were afraid to use it inside the tent in case we gassed ourselves.

The next morning we set off at 4.00 am, but that was still not early enough. By eight o'clock the sun had caught us. Mick stopped every five paces to rest his helmeted head on the snow, like a pilgrim. My trailing rope was getting damp and heavy. By midday the purgatory had become a burning white hell. Deep sugar snow, blinding sun.

"Mick, I think we must simply have a brew . . . croak. Col over there, looks flat."

"Groan . . . croak . . . okay . . . gasp."

Mick unpacked his stove, which looked as if it had not survived the ice axe attack, and began melting water. Above us the Headwall filled the sky. I was beginning to have nightmarish thoughts about our situation. This easy ridge had been deceptively serious, with cliffs on both sides. Big cliffs. And looking up, I did not like the look of

154

the Headwall. It was too steep. The lower section, snow-covered slabs, was increasingly menacing. I tried thinking of other things . . . the sun.

"The sun rose, having no alternative, into the nothing new."

"Whassat?" said Mick.

"Beckett. It's from *Murphy*," I said. "The next sentence is 'Murphy sat out of it.' Which seems like a good idea. Let's get the tent up. What d'you think?"

We had stopped at a near perfect bivouac site, except for one murderous flaw, which was not to become apparent for two days.

"This really is the most perfectly useless mountain tent," I began again, as I helped Mick erect the object of my scorn.

"I don't think so, especially at £100. Know what I mean?" said Mick, tapping his nose with a forefinger. It was a habit peculiar to Mick at that time, and quite contagious. By the end of the expedition we were all doing it.

"Well, it doesn't have a bell end, so you can't cook except right inside, and that's probably fatal. You have nowhere to leave your rucksack in a storm, except on your sleeping bag, and that's useless. There are no belay loops, so you have to cut great holes in the fabric to belay through . . . "

"But it's a cuddly little tent," said Mick.

"It's an absolute cheek calling it a mountain tent. I bet the designer has never set foot on a mountain." I was not to be diverted so easily. Probably I felt about the tent much as Mick felt about his rucksack.

We spent the afternoon trying to escape the penetrating rays by draping our sleeping bags over the tent. Brew followed brew. Mick read *Gorky Park*. I tried to mend my cracked finger tips. The problem with eczema on the hands, is that altitude, cold and low humidity seem to make it much worse. I wrapped sticky tape round each digit. John, an eczema specialist, had recommended

Superglue.

"Superglue?"

"Yes, it's very good for the cracks, but you have to do it every day. When I tell them in the clinic I am going to Superglue their cracks they think I am joking, but they soon stop laughing when I produce the tube!" I could imagine.

The next day was rather special. The alarm started twittering about 2.00 am. We were packed and away by four. There was a difficult step at the end of the Snow Arête and we roped up for the first time since the glacier for eighty feet of crumbling stone piled into a shape like giant hands clasped in prayer, dotted with whipped snow, which we had to clear with great sweeps of the arm. Plodding into the deepening snow, we realised that we were at last on the Hangengletscher, on almost flat ground. Six am, we had beaten the sun. Tent, brew, and sleep for two hours. At 8.45 we left the tent, and plodded uphill towards the Headwall. The slope steepened until we had to use our ice axes. I was still trying to avert my eyes from our project, muttering to myself, "Definitely going to settle down, family man, easy trips with Maggie and lots of children. And a garden. Gardens take up a lot of time. Can't possibly leave the garden for long enough to climb big peaks any more. Top of ice at last . . . three breaths . . . better than yesterday with full sacks . . . counted fifteen breaths per step . . . "

Crossing the bergschrund by an avalanche cone, we followed the runnel caused by the stream of snow. It was easier going, slightly icy. A long finger of rock reached down from the Headwall, I aimed for its tip. This would be the test. Would it be granite? Or the same rotten piles that made up the difficult step? Would there be natural runner placements? Or would the rock demand something brave of us? I brushed a sliver of snow away from the surface, and revealed a perfect peg-sized crack. The Stubby Angle (sadly no longer made) slipped in about a third of the way, and a few firm taps of the ice hammer drove the rest of the peg up to its eye. Textbook stuff.

"This has got to be a good omen, Mick." Mick led through. When he was far enough for me to have to shout, I asked, "What's it like?"

"Gasp . . . give me a chance . . . to answer . . . gasp . . . looks okay. I am climbing the ice in the back of a groove. Long as it lasts, we're okay . . . in trouble if it runs out though."

Although Mick finished the pitch in thirty minutes, he spent an hour looking for a belay. It is always this way, you pass perfect belays, but never at 150-foot intervals. When I joined him on the belay, he said the climbing was so good, he was actually enjoying his first technical Himalayan pitch. Half an hour later, I was scratching about, trying to find a good runner, when I hammered an ice-filled crack, and a plate of rock came away. I trapped it against my knees, but could not hold it.

"Belowwww! Below! Rock! Below!" The plate seemed to float in the air, and was drifting away from Mick, then it glanced off a bulge and crashed into his leg.

"Oh . . . Owww! . . . ahh!"

"Are you all right, Mick? Shall I come down?"

"No, no! Go on!" Then in a lower voice, "Only two pitches up, and already he tries to kill me."

From the top of my pitch we fixed the 300 feet of rope I had been hauling, and abseiled down to the snow slope, off the end of the rope, then slip-slid back to the tent, happy that there was some prospect of being able to climb that monster after all.

The blitter of our synchronised alarm watches woke us at 2.00 am. It was time to go down. We left a snow shovel and a depressingly small payload of pegs and rope at the Hangengletscher. Below the difficult step, Mick followed our old tracks diagonally across the slope to the bivouac. I could see him below, lying on his rucksack, waiting for me. As I followed, I stepped slightly above our track, and there was a loud 'oomph!' from the slope.

Mick said, "I wonder how dangerous those noises are, whether the slope is really close to avalanching or not. You hear it all the time in the Alps."

"Very dangerous. There's a thin crack above, right across the slope."

I stepped down below the old tracks, and almost immediately there was another 'oomph!' and a crack opened up across the entire slope below my feet. The crack widened as the slope began to move. At first the snow slid as a single sheet, then it folded and buckled, and finally broke up into a writhing mass as it slid out of sight. Mick scrambled backwards like a crab to the safety of a rock island. I staggered down to him as quickly as my rucksack and the dangling hardware would allow.

"Lobby and Bruce?" asked Mick.

I looked at my watch. "4.59 am. They said they would start at four, so they should be in the First Tower Gully now."

"Right in the path of the avalanche."

"Let's just get down, Mick. There's nothing we can do about them."

The avalanche track formed a ribbon sixty-five feet wide, the length of the Snow Arête. The entire Arête had lost its top six inches, we waded down the sugary wake. About half way down, Mick said he could make out a blue shape on the far moraine, a tent. Later there was a figure waving. I waved back. Worry and, I must admit guilt, evaporated. I had not killed my friends after all.

Phil and Bruce had indeed set their alarm for 4.00 am, but an instinct to remain in the cosy warm sleeping bags, overtook them. Their next alarm was the roar of the avalanche, which had been silent to us. Soon afterwards they saw us alive and descending. Phil had stayed on the moraine to watch us down.

Meanwhile, John and Liz had climbed on the proposed descent spur, and had been having a dreadful time with the deep soft snow, and a malfunctioning stove. They had just packed their tent for a tactical retreat, when Liz heard the rumble, and they saw an enormous avalanche engulf the Snow Arête, pouring off it at the sides like a surfacing submarine. John and Liz were so sure that Mick and I had been caught, that they spent the next twenty minutes searching the debris for signs, till John saw a pair of figures "scampering down as fast as possible".

Mick and I clanked down, dangling hardware like cow bells. The crack had been very close. The distance between life and death was no thicker than a cigarette paper. If I had not left our tracks, Mick would have probably been taken with the slope when he continued. If he had not waited for me, if the crack above me had opened . . . if . . . if . . .

The life at Base had a rhythm anchored to the stream. Rajab made a water chute to wash the pans under. Soon after we arrived the stream stopped running at night, then it started a little later each morning. Our water source, a snow drift, had been the size of a soccer pitch when we arrived. Now it was down to a tennis court. There was a ceremony called watching the First Water. We waited with tooth brushes and paste, soap and towel. When we returned from the Pillar, the First Water flowed over Rajab's chute at 12.40. Rajab predicted the stream would dry up completely in one week. After First Water, Bruce and Iqbal made their first ever chapatis. All of Iqbal's chapatis looked like maps, and this led to discussion and argument, while all of Bruce's chapatis looked like cucumbers and pears. They tasted the same.

Meanwhile Rajab made a delicious dhal and rice, which we ate with tinned fish. I had learned to detest dhal after the previous expeditions. Now I was being re-educated. Rajab's cooking, like all fine cuisine, encouraged conversation.

"What is this brown rice?" Iqbal asked, looking up from his book.

"It was invented in California, is eaten in Europe, is said to be healthy, and tastes like cardboard."

"But I do like brown macaroni," Liz said.

"I don't," said John, "and I prefer white bread, sliced."

Mick became restless after a day at Base, though my aging and rheumatic limbs were still complaining. But if we were to make an impression on the mountain, we had to go up again. This time, our objective was the Descent Spur. We staggered up the moraine after lunch, nicely bloated on Rajab's filled parathas (stuffed with corned beef, potato, and petit pois), followed by a stiff semolina, flavoured with cardomoms and raisins. Phil and Bruce had also made a second dessert, wild rhubarb stewed in sugar.

The idea was simple. By climbing the Descent Spur to the summit plateau, we would acclimatise to 19,500 feet, while at the same time inspecting our route of descent. It was a good idea but, like so many good ideas on this trip, had a small defect. We could not climb the spur. We barely reached the apex of the English-Allen Prominence, where John and Liz had given up two days earlier. The final tower of the Prominence was about 1300 feet above the glacier. We decided to turn it on the left. Mick was about to step across an avalanche runnel, when a warning boulder hurtled down it like a bob sleigh. Mick withdrew his boot, and a huge rockfall spewed out of a cave in the tower, boulders the size of filing cabinets bouncing out of the runnel below us. After about five minutes the crescendo diminished to a few pebbles and sand.

Looking up, I said, "I suppose it might look stable now, but I am not risking it. I'm going to see if there is another way on the right."

"I think I'll wait a few minutes, then go this way."

Thinks: Obviously not a family man . . .

We met again on the Prominence, where we shook hands. Above the Tower the snow was just awful, very similar to the structure that had avalanched on the Snow

Arête, six inches of crust overlying bottomless sugar. The crust almost supports you, even appears to think about it seriously, then at the last moment, after you have committed your entire weight to the step, it decides it's no good. And lets you down to your thighs.

Meanwhile Bruce and Phil were planning to visit the Hangengletscher, but diarrhoea struck first. Afterwards Bruce explained, "Lob's not well, he is looking green, and very, very old."

Liz left Base to do more of her pencil drawings of the Pillar, of the Pap of Girgindil, and other salient peaks. She took John along with her on these excursions. And Iqbal climbed Melangush again, this time with George.

Phil had recovered when we returned from the English-Allen Prominence. I needed to escape a little so, after breakfast, Phil and I climbed up to a ruined shepherd's enclosure, high on Melangush Chish. I took pencils and a note book, Phil his camera. We would sketch and name the surrounding peaks.

Peak 6575m on the Polish map (made in 1976 by Jerzy Wala) was a delicate snowy thing, a kind of Pap of Miar. The main Miar peaks peeped over its shoulder. There was a growling peak at the head of the Barpu Glacier, which we noted down as Barpu Peak, but later Ibrahim told me the local name was Dascaram Chish. I drew profiles of the horizon, adding observations and notes from the map.

We sat in the weak sun, sheltered from the north wind by the ruin, watching lenticular clouds grow behind Polan Peak, east of Polan La. Ragged clouds streamed in the lee of the Golden Pillar like prayer flags. By our feet plants were poking out from the snow margins. They had endured a long winter, their growing season would be no more than eight weeks, possibly less. The flowers here were white, yellow and blue, not a single red. Above us – winter, on the west-facing slopes between us and Base Camp – spring. The south-facing slopes, towards Miar, had reached high summer, exultant life, thick with Alpine

161

colonies and forests of scrub willow. There was noise, too, buzzings, low and high, the squawk of a curious chough, and distant warblings from something too shy to show itself; quick movements under a leaf and in the shade maybe a spider. Far away a rumbling rockfall and the distant thunder of an avalanche – the Himalayan Symphony.

On 29th July, George, John and Liz left the expedition after breakfast and the rest of us suddenly knew the fun was over, the serious times had arrived. Now we would have to make our first attempt to climb the Pillar. I was depressed, and a little bit scared. Mick and I spent the morning putting our hill food into plastic bags. We had got the weight per man-day of food down to 250 grams. Even so, the food and gas came to ten kilos of unwelcome extra weight. That night, learning from our mistakes, we left Hewitt's at 10.00 pm, and reached the Hangengletscher in one push, pushing, I could not help noticing, twenty-five-kilo sacks. The weather deteriorated throughout the day until horrid squalls tried to blow the tent away with us still inside. We spent the time sleeping, brewing, and brushing our boots clean of snow, so we could bring them inside the inadequate tent. Each of our plastic bags was numbered. Some contained date bars, so were slightly heavier than bags with Crunchy bars, which would be saved till last. There was also a bag labelled 'Emergency', which contained soup cubes, and Paracetamol. I celebrated my brother's birthday with an extra brew of soup from our emergency bag.

The next day it continued to snow all day. I had remembered to bring John's Superglue, only to find the cap had cracked and bonded itself back, so the glue, when squeezed, squirted out of a small tear in the base, bonding everything within range. I spent the period between Ready-brek (breakfast) and the date bar (lunch) prising my fingers apart, so that I could throw the tube away. Mick had already become despondent about the weather and begun to develop a nasty cough. I knew that I would soon be coughing too. Like a pair of Siamese twins, we must necessarily share each other's diseases and infections, while living in a tent the size of a bed. We learned from the radio that Phil and Bruce were stuck in the same conditions on the First Tower.

The strain was not so much in putting up with the constant snow, but in sustaining the hope that the weather might clear.

I wrote in my notebook, "All we need is half a day of sun on the face to clear it of the powder. But we need it now. We have lots of food, enough for a week of waiting, but Mick will be mad long before that."

With our down clothing and massive sleeping bags, there was barely room to breathe in a tent six feet by four feet. The rucksacks had to live outside. Each night they would disappear under the fresh fall of snow. I too began to grow depressive after the third day. It was difficult to imagine the climb succeeding now. It was Iqbal we felt really sorry for. He had worked so hard to get onto this trip, and now would have precious little mountaineering to show for it. He had to badger the Pakistani government for months, and eventually they foisted him off on us, presumably to teach us both a lesson.

By the fourth day, Mick was muttering to himself. "Never again . . . never. The thing that really gets me down," explained Mick, "is the boredom. I couldn't even be bothered to put in my contact lenses today . . . Phew . . . It's so boring . . . What time is it now? Is that all? Gawd, this is so boring."

After a long silence, broken only by his mutterings, Mick asked, "When is the sabbath here?"

"Friday, and half Saturday. Why?"

"I'm wondering if the PIA offices will be closed."

"They should be open every day. Today is Saturday."

"Hmmm . . . I am just thinking about when I've got to leave, sensibly."

I had instant visions of Michael leaving insensibly, throwing beer at the airport staff, and roaring at the top of his voice, "I am a respectable civil servant but I am on holiday . . . whoopeeee." Meanwhile Mick was chuntering on.

"I've got this flight booked for the 16th, which is five weeks' holiday. I could take an extra week, but that would be mega-bad news because I need four days off in December for the Irish lecture tour. Plus PIA probably need three days to reconfirm the flight for the 23rd so I would only gain four days if I missed that flight."

"Hey, look! Sunshine!" We blundered out of the tent, but the sun disappeared again.

Mick said, "I have no doubt it will snow again in five minutes, but if tomorrow is good, I shall be so pleased . . . so pleased, I shall walk round the tent in small circles!"

It snowed. On day five of our incarceration, Mick said he had to go down for his sanity. Funny thing that, I had assumed all these years that it was too late. On the way down the First Tower we met up with Phil and Bruce. Phil too had been keeping a diary:

Day 1 Reached bivi on First Tower
Day 2 No entry
Day 3 No entry
Day 4 No entry
Day 5 Still effing snowing

When we all returned to Base, Rajab had news of George, Liz and John. George had had a close shave with a bear. On the walk down to Hoppar rocks had rolled past him and the porters and, when they looked up, they saw the bear. It was seven feet tall, green and fond of ghee. I don't know how Rajab knew about the ghee.

It had been snowing at Base, too, but the next day the sun shone, and the thin sprinkling evaporated. Base Camp was now surrounded by summer foliage. The hillsides were covered in flowers, like forty-five-degree meadows, no grasses, just very thick colonies of green stems, and open leaves. Clusters of shimmering flower heads, in yellow and blue, natural pointillism, gilded the slopes into the distance. The plants seemed to have leaves from one British species and flowers from another. We referred to them accordingly; there was the bracken-pea, the camomile-sage, the forget-me-not-mint, which smelled of lemon geranium, and the buttercup-rue.

13

Time and optimism were draining away when on Wednesday, 5th August the weather began to turn. Mick and I had been back at Base for two nights. We packed slowly and deliberately, checking and rechecking each article, knowing that this would be our last chance; and when we had packed and repacked our sacks, tidied up the tent, laid out our clothes, and there were no more displacement activities left, Mick and I left the comforts of Base with twenty-five-kilo loads. I half enjoyed the walk up to Hewitt's Camp, perhaps in anticipation of the brutish nastiness to come. While we walked the sky was fickle. First clear, then ominous, then squally, and finally at dusk, when we reached the camp, promising again. When we breakfasted at midnight, it was overcast, but an hour later when we had crossed the glacier, the stars had lit up the black sky like a distant city.

The glacier at this point was barely 14,800 feet above sea level. For us this was rather bad news, it left about 8250 feet of climbing between us and the summit. We had compared the Pillar to the Walker Spur, but in reality it was as large as two Walkers.

For the third time, we soloed up the First Tower, separated from each other by the blackness, each working in our private pool of light. The climbing was straightforward. The main difficulties were two thirty-foot walls of ice and some steep ground between. I kept close to Mick to reduce the energy of the ice and loose rocks he inadvertently knocked down. By the time we reached the crest of the Tower, a faint dawn had begun to unfold the mountain. There had been heavy snow since we last visited the Snow Arête, and we worried that it would be too deep for us. We were lucky although it looked deep and even, near the crest we could feel our old tracks under the surface, like stepping stones. We spent the rest of the night and the early morning balancing upwards and feeling for the next step. When we reached our old bivouac site at the Hangengletscher, Mick could no longer hold back nature's ordinary functions. He dropped his pants, took a long stride off our hidden tracks, and promptly disappeared from view.

"You really ought to keep to the tracks, Mick, know what I mean?" (Tap-tap).

"Sod off, Saunders!"

At seven o'clock the sun burst through the array of pinnacles leading up to the Golden Pillar. There was one shard of stone in particular that always caught our attention, a golden finger indicating "This is the way." There is a famous boulder you can see from the Eigerwand, on the verge of toppling off the North-West Ridge. That boulder is an open challenge to problemists, especially on the side that overhangs the Rot Flu. This Golden Finger throws out the same challenge.

After the Five-Day Ordeal we had buried bags of food by the old bivouac site, together with ropes and climbing gear. Mick was digging the food out of the snow.

"What's for lunch?" I leant out of the tent.

"Coffee and half a Crunchy bar?"

"Okay. We'll have the Ready-brek for supper."

It is a bit of a joke calling that thin broth supper, but you don't get to eat much if you have to carry the food as well as a megaton of climbing gear. Though we had got the food down to 250 grams each per day, Mick and I weren't proud of this achievement, we simply could not carry more.

On the 7th, Day 2, the climbing started with the two fixed pitches. The plan was to climb the entire Slabs in one day. In Britain we had based our aspirations on the telephotograph John had taken from Bojohaghur. It was impossible to say how hard the climbing might be. So we did the sensible thing and took lots of fixing rope, 10mm polypropylene sailing rope. Most of this ended up as bakhshish to the porters, though we did manage to fix 300 feet on what turned out to be the easiest 300 feet of the climb. No sooner had we left the fixed rope than the Pillar began to show its teeth. The great drools of ice streaking the Slabs became ice-filled cracks, the névé became powder. Higher again, the cracks closed up and, under the powder, the edges sloped out.

The Slabs were about a thousand feet long. We had worked out a line that seemed to follow ice streaks. The line was disconnected by short walls and overhangs. At first we thought the crucial bits would be getting over the walls to regain the icy streaks. As we climbed higher, the reverse became true.

The next seven or eight pitches we found increasingly difficult. Mick crossed a wall via an overhung ramp to gain a section of Slabs above me. I was belayed too close to the wall to see him. But I could trace his progress. Like bubbles from a diver, rivulets of snow drifted over the edge. I knew the climbing had got thin when the rivulet dried up for a long time. I was wearing a duvet and extra thick belaying gloves, but still grew cold.

"Vic?" Mick's voice was tense. "There's no ice here. I think there might be a streak to my left, but the Slabs are blank. I am going to try to tension across. Watch the rope!"

I watched it like a hawk. The rivulets poured over the overhang, edging slowly towards me. At last a deluge of powder and gravel poured over the belay, and down my neck. Mick had reached his stance.

By late afternoon we had made good progress and put

ten pitches behind us which accounted for most of the Slabs. But there had been no ledges or any possible bivouac site. We met in the base of the feature we called the Amphitheatre. It was really very like the Spider, a sloping icy stage, a monstrously intimidating backdrop, and great cliffs falling out of sight towards the valley.

"Mick?" (We tended to call to each other by name, even though no one else could possibly have answered.) "This is superb. It is worth it, isn't it, all that waiting and effort?"

"Might be, let's see when we get up, Vic."

"Any sign of a bivi site yet?"

Mick is eagle-eyed when it comes to the home comforts, and he had spotted a bit of flake we could excavate. There wasn't another ledge for miles. We sat beside each other and pulled the tent over us like a big bag. As sitting bivis go, it was truly luxurious. The stove was on Mick's side, so I had the pleasure of dozing while he made the morning brew. It took us two hours to brew, dress, pack the tent away, and sort out the ropes, which were frozen and handled like wire hawser. I was shivering by the time Mick led off the next pitch. After a few yards on the dense hard ice, Mick stopped, placed an ice screw, and began to fiddle with his gloves. I felt very cold and very impatient.

"What's the problem?" I shouted.

"Got to get my gloves off. Fingers are frozen." Mick massaged his hands and stuck them inside his jacket.

The climbing across the Amphitheatre was not steep, but the ice was so hard that the crampons and axes did not bite more than a fraction of an inch. It felt insecure. On the far side there seemed to be two possible lines, and both were thin, only just threading a way through the overhanging walls. The one on the right we could see most of, and it looked uncompromisingly steep. The alternative, a gully directly above was less steep where we would see, but the top half was out of view. We chose this line, with typical ostrich logic. The gully turned into a chimney. Mick was engrossed in the work. Gravel and powder ricocheted down, and I tried to hide in a shallow scoop. Mick had been stopped by an overhang. He was bridged out, peering upward. His crampons made horrid scraping noises. He had managed to place two wobbly pegs, but he could not clip the sling into them. The sling, which was round his neck, had caught under his hood.

Mick was screaming, "You effing sling, get off my effing neck you effing sling."

I really thought he would fall out of the chimney in frustration. I nearly did when I followed. As I approached the belay I could see he was grinning from ear to ear. He must be pleased with the lead, I thought. But no, he was belayed on black shale.

"It's just like Devon, Vic!" he burbled while I removed the runners by pulling out the flakes they hung round.

"Just look up there, Vic!"

The next pitch was the continuation of the shale dyke. It formed a vertical black stripe, a shallow chimney of loose flakes, frozen in a glaze of clear ice.

"Oh, err, looks good," I hoped somewhat doubtfully. I was beginning to have unpleasant memories of some of Mick's favourite West Country shale cliffs. There were no runners in the Shale Chimney, no nice friendly cracks or spikes. Very precariously I tiptoed upwards on the points of my crampons. After half-an-hour's work I was looking down ninety feet of free-hanging rope.

It's best to calm down . . . breathe nice and slow. It is also easier if you can get runners in, the inner voice went on.

But watch the cramp, don't stop too long – another, dissenting, inner voice.

Get a runner in . . . now – the first voice again.

Can't, not safe to stop – the dissenting voice.

Slow down . . . one breath at a time.

Quick, that pedestal before the cramp sets in.

Stop! . . . Hurry! . . . Careful! The voices were arguing. I had a terrible headache by the time I fixed the belay.

The Shale Chimney led to the right-hand edge of the Pillar, but we were now in a sea of mist. At midday it began to snow. We needed to see clearly to pick the line through the complicated walls above, so we stopped for a brew. The packet of instant chocolate sprinkled onto the panful of slush was delicious. It began to snow heavily by 2.30 pm and we decided to bivouac. We would make an early start the next day, we hoped.

We were lucky, it stopped snowing some time during the night and the morning of the 8th was grey, but visibility was good enough for our purposes. This day would, we hoped, lead us out of the heart of the Pillar. Somewhere above was the Giant Jammed Block, guarded by gently overhanging walls which were breached by a wide and tiresome chimney, leading in turn to a large and perfectly flat ledge on top of the GJ Block. It would have made a magnificent bivi site.

"What a pity it is only twelve o'clock," said Mick when we got there.

"Let's stop for a brew anyway." We felt free to take off our sacks without tying them into the belay.

"Only problem is," I said after a while, "how in hell's name are we going to get out of here?" I was beginning to get bad feelings about the place. We were completely walled in.

"It does seem to be wonderfully overhanging ... everywhere." Mick was admiring our plight. "But we could try to peg that crack over there. Great, eh?" This was not very reassuring, but what can you do when you're with someone who insists on enjoying himself when you're frightened?

Mick tried to climb the crack with his rucksack on, it was impossible, so he came down, left the sack with me, and tried again. He reached high, placed a peg in the rock, pushing it as far as it would go, reached for his ice hammer, and hammered the peg till the tone went up half an octave. The peg began to ring. I love the clear sound of

171

well driven steel. It is like the smooth finish a sharp plane leaves on timber. Then he clipped one of the ropes into the peg and shouted.

"Pull tight on red!"

I pulled as hard as I could, and Mick rose effortlessly up the wall. He clipped his harness into the peg and prepared to repeat the entire process. This technique had been pioneered in the 'twenties. Aid climbing had come a long way since then.

"Mick," I shouted, "Mick, yes, you! You know that no one aids like this any more, don't you?"

"But it's the only way I know . . . now, HAUL! HAUL! HAUL!"

The Aid Pitch gave us access to the ledges leading to what we called the Shield. It was a crucial section of the route, for, up to the Amphitheatre we had been on the front of the Pillar, from there to the Giant Jammed Block the route followed the right-hand edge, but the key to the exit was, we hoped, the right wall of the Pillar, where we had seen from Base Camp thin lines of snow leading towards the top. What we weren't sure of was what happened where the thin lines disappeared. The feature that particularly exercised our imaginations was the Shield. The ledges seemed to run out near the bottom of the Shield, and start again near its top. The connection turned out to be a smooth-sided chimney. It was just wide enough to squeeze an arm and leg into, and it was very, very steep.

"Mick, I am going to have to leave my sack here," I shouted when I reached the base of the chimney. Even without a sack, the chimney was hard. It required a kind of eel-like squirming. The knees and crampons scraped and slid on the smooth rock.

"Mick, it is quite . . . pant . . . hard." My ice axes were dangling round my feet. Bloody axes . . . groan, pant . . . get out of the way! "Mick, sorry. Finding it hard . . . pant, groan."

"You seem to be going up!"

"Yes, it's because I am too frightened . . . wheeze pant . . . to stay still. Blast, you stupid ice axe . . . " It had caught in my crampons. "Get out of it! . . . urgh . . . wheeze push pant . . . argh." Result: another inch. In the thin air I could barely breathe. "I am making some progress, Mick . . . pant wheeze . . . nearly there."

The runner was fifty feet below me now. If I was to fall it would be at least a hundred feet before the rope could catch me, assuming Mick's belay was adequate. Don't think about it . . . squirm pant . . . hargh. "I am there, Mick!" And looking for a belay. God, there must be one. It's late. Where's the bivi site? We've got to get a move on. There, a peg, oh dear, it seems to come out when I pull. Push it back in. Clip. There was nothing better, so I wedged myself in the top of the chimney. "Okay, Mick, on belay, only don't fall off!"

When Mick passed me, he was forced to step on the loose peg. He let out a blood-curdling yell as it twisted out of the crack.

"For God's sake, Mick, go easy."

The really chilling thought, though, was the knowledge that this was an irreversible section. No safe pegs equals no abseil. In bad weather we could not climb down. We might not be able to even in good weather.

It was twilight when Mick's voice drifted over the mist. I followed his pitch as quickly as I could, taking out the loose pegs with a finger through the eye. Dusk falls quickly in these latitudes. I reached the stance in the dark. "What's the chance of a bivi, Mick?"

"Zero. We could try cutting a ledge here." There were perhaps four inches of ice stuck on the rock.

"But it's useless."

"There is nothing else."

"What's the belay?"

"It's a good nut."

"Just one?"

"Nothing else."

We got the tent out and hung it like a big bag. Getting inside was not easy. We took turns at looking on while the other slowly bundled his things in. We were cold, tired and tense. Both our headtorches failed at the same time. Soon it began snowing and the spindrift poured down the huge walls above in waves, engulfing our microcosm. It was not much of an ecological niche. Mick thought it would be a good idea to spend the night hanging in his harness. I thought it better to stand in my rucksack all night. Both methods had defects; Mick's belay was stable but tended to cut the flow of blood to his legs; my belay allowed the free circulation of blood but, because the sack was tied to the rope, every time I dozed off, my feet shot into the air and I slumped onto the rope with a jerk and a lot of bad language.

It snowed gently all night – I know because I was awake. Inside the tent, we heard and felt the regular rush of the spindrift buffeting us like surf. The tent fabric pressed against our faces, crusty with ice. The pressure was uncomfortable. When it became too much Mick unzipped his corner of the tent, buckets of powder snow poured in through the opening before he had time to zip it up. The zip became stuck and more snow poured in, straight into his sleeping bag.

"You damned effing zip. Why do you have to jam now?" . . . etc. etc. It was rather a long night.

When at last the alarm went off at 3.30 am we were unusually pleased. Mick said, "Well, Vic, we seem to be surviving."

"The basis of optimism is sheer terror," I replied.

"Eh?"

"Oscar Wilde."

By the time the morning had taken the razor's edge off the cold, we had succeeded in reaching the final line of ramps. The situation was superb. We were surrounded by acres of rock. Above us the towering Headwall, below the rock falling in walls and slabs towards the glacier 5000 feet below. We hoped it was going to be straightforward ice climbing now. All we had to do was follow the snowy diagonal across the Headwall, and that was it. True, at the far end the diagonal ramp was blocked by an open book corner. True, the corner was overhung by a monstrous ear-shaped sérac, but surely the end was in sight. Please.

"Well, Mick, last lap now." I set off happily along the ramp. After about fifteen feet, it got through to me that this was going to be another trying pitch. The Headwall leant over the ramp and the ramp itself was a narrow, outward-sloping ledge. But the powder lying over the ramp covered no ice or cracks, just smooth sloping rock. Oh, well, I'll just ease my foot onto this patch of snow and hope it doesn't move . . . now . . . gently . . . push the axe into the corner, not too hard or it will slide away, breathe easy . . .

After an hour I had led out 120 feet of rope with no runners. Once again, I found myself wondering how good Mick's belay was. He must be getting cold, I thought. Pray God I don't get cramp now. I can't move any quicker. My muscles are aching . . . need oxygen. Don't relax. Stop shaking, leg. I was gradually losing control of my body. Come on, just two feet more. A crack . . . peg . . . get a peg in! Now, quickly! It was difficult to keep my balance while holding the peg and bashing it into the crack. At last I was able to shout down, "I'm safe, Mick."

I suppose in all the effort I had not noticed the Ice Ear. It was now almost overhead. We had seen this feature from Base Camp and thought its apparent shape must be a trick of perspective. It was much bigger than we had imagined, a massive sérac, high as a five-storey building, the whole edifice leaning out over the Open-Book Corner with no apparent means of support. Each successive pitch brought the Ear closer, until it filled the sky.

The Open-Book Corner was vertical. The snow-filled

cracks offered no security. Mick cleaned the snow out of the cracks as he climbed. There was a masterly rhythm: move up, clean the cracks; move up, clean; move up, clean. When Mick finished, it looked as if the corner had been hoovered. All the time I shivered on a tiny ledge, showered with the debris of Mick's progress and looking up at the bewildering underside of the sérac. The outcome did not seem to be in doubt for a minute, and when I followed I knew I had been watching a virtuoso display.

The alarm rang at 3.30 am on 10th August, but we did not hear it. Our tent was pitched on top of the Ear. We were enjoying our first night on horizontal ground for five days. The grand plan included taking up the tent and all our gear to a convenient point near the summit, dropping the sacks for a summit stroll, and picking them up on the way down to the descent ridge, but it had come as a shock after the Corner to find the snow so deep we could barely reach the plateau. The revised grand plan was to leave the tent and all the gear, except a single rope and a stove, climb to the summit and return to the Ear for a second bivouac. We set out at 6.00 am, thigh-deep in powder.

"You go first, Mick, I can't sort out the ropes. They're frozen into knots."

"Mumble . . . complain . . . moan . . . I'm gonna be slow . . . mumble . . . "

A few minutes later Mick sat in the snow and was kicking his feet in the air.

"What on earth?"

"My feet, they're freezing." He thought it was a good idea to warm his feet every twenty minutes after this. Each time he hurled himself onto his back, and kicked the air, I could only look on amazed. After an hour we had made almost no progress. We kept walking into an invisible snowdrift. The surface did not change but the snow became chest deep. We executed a series of flanking movements and each time came up against the same invisible barrier.

"Mick, if this goes on much longer, we won't be able to reach the descent ridge, let alone the summit." Mick didn't reply. We were pushed half a kilometer off course when the invisible snow drift ended as suddenly as it had begun. To regain the crest of the ridge, we now had to cross a sérac barrier. A steep snow wall turned the barrier on its left, but, God, what a battle. The snow was bottomless. Nothing seemed to work. The Wilkinson Method, the Kneeling Technique, the Trench and the Crawl all failed after a few inches. We spent enough energy on that snow wall to light up New York. We were not in the mood to give up; not now. Not after a week of hard and exhausting climbing. We were definitely not going to be beaten by a sixty foot snow wall. At last, after what was probably the psychological crux of the route, we found the going easier, and reached the crest of the ridge in mist. We were a mile and a quarter from the tent, it was late morning and we still had a thousand yards and the summit cone before us. Exhaustion and the need for a clear patch to see the summit indicated a tea-stop.

"Look, it's cleared." Mick pointed with the pan.

"That must be the summit. Pass me the brew."

"Doesn't look far now."

"Please let it be close."

"Yes," said Mick. "I promise it will be no more than two hours."

"Promise?" I asked.

"Yes, promise, if you go first. Know what I mean?" He was tapping his nose again. Just for that I drained the last few drops of coffee.

After the rest, when no more excuses could be found, I said, "Shall we climb the front, or round the back?" referring to the summit cone.

"Round the back," said Mick. "It's always easier round the back."

More ostrich logic.

An hour later we had reached the cone and were pushing round the back, waist-deep. There was an umph, and the snow settled an inch lower around me. A fine crescent-shaped crack appeared in the snow above.

"Get back, Mick, and careful. We are going to have to go for the front after all."

"Can't we try this rock rib, here?"

"No, you try if you like, I'm going back to the front."

We were too tired to argue. When I led the way back, Mick just followed. It took another ninety minutes of purgatory to reach the top which was about the size of a sitting room. I took photos of Mick and he of me. Using the elastic from my mitts, I fixed the camera to the ice axe, and just managed to collapse beside Mick as the shutter went off. Usually I get pictures of my backside.

We took photographs of Nanga Parbat, Diran, the Ultar group and Trivor. But from the east, where Kunyang Chish should have been, massive cloud banks blacked out the sky. This was disappointing as the encyclopaedic Pole, Kowalewski, had sent us an excellent panorama taken in 1970 from Kunyang Chish and I had wanted to return the favour. But I was still supremely happy to be standing with Mick on the summit of Spantik, the deliverance of six days' climbing and an idea that had been conceived thirty-six months before. Now we had to get off the mountain alive and the weather was going to make it a race.

14

We had barely got off the summit cone and down to the small triangle of rock where we had left the rope and rucksack, when the first squalls overtook us. The temperature dropped suddenly. Something in our tired, dulled brains said, "Go, and go now." Hoisting our weary bodies up, we began to follow our tracks. After half an hour I felt the first trickle of the static electricity, so did Mick. There was a growing buzzing noise. We lay down and tried to bury ourselves in the snow, to hide from the electric rain, but the storm had strengthened, so after five minutes of ostriching, we decided that being stuck on the summit plateau was perhaps an even more serious threat. So we pressed on, trying to make ourselves as inconspicuous as possible. The flurries and squalls brought drifting snow. Our tracks disappeared. The horizons vanished, all I could see of Mick, who was ten feet away, was a shadowy outline. We were on a 23,000-foot plateau, surrounded by precipices. And we could not know which way to go. Bivouacking on the plateau seemed most unattractive. We simply had to rediscover our tracks, it was the only route through the séracs. I knelt down and prodded the slope with my axe. Here and there was a softness, which I took to be our snow-filled tracks. Like blind men we felt our way down, searching for the tell-tale hollows under the smooth, seamless, perfect surface. We crawled on our hands and knees for a mile and a quarter, prodding and feeling. It was slow work. The

179

wind whipped noisily at our clothing. It was hard to speak, not only over the competing noise, but also because the cold was locking our faces and lips. Mick voiced our common fear.

"Ve tent . . . I don' think i' was ver' well anchored . . . hope i's still vere . . . " Visions of it flying down to Base Camp in advance of us flashed past my mind. But the tent was still faithfully waiting for us.

The next morning it took us until 6.30 to leave the bivouac site. We were slow and decrepit after seven days without proper food and rest. Mick coughed violently, and spat out a strip of throat. Coughs were affecting us both, badly. Mick could no longer shout at me, and I could not yawn. Mick thought it was the altitude, but I felt sure we were suffering infections. Our bodies were falling to bits.

During the night the weather had regained its composure and now it was clear and very cold. Below us a sea of cloud filled the valleys, which was worrying, because we could not be sure where we were to leave the plateau if we could not see the Descent Spur. During the climb we had noted a tongue of plateau stretching out over the ridge. On this Tongue lay some ice blocks which we referred to as the Crumbs on the Tongue. Slowly we made our tired way uphill, following our track of the previous day till we were able to diverge and follow the edge of the plateau towards the Descent Spur, or at least towards where we thought it should be, our feet insensible with cold, like lumps of wood. At about 9.00 we stopped for a radio call, a vague crackling which might have been Lobby. This was big slot country, crevasses big enough to sink a battleship, hiding under blankets of innocent snow. Mick and I walked down separated by the full fifty yards of our rope to give us maximum warning if anything should happen.

After three worrying hours of crossing the high plateau we arrived at the top of an icefall. There below us were the

Crumbs. The valley fog was receding and the Tongue was revealed, but where on its edge was the descent? If we picked the wrong spot, not only would we miss the Spur, but also be abseiling over large séracs into space. Descending the icefall involved making our first ever snow bollard abseils. Mick was extremely suspicious about this novel technique. Being too tired to worry, I went first, and almost immediately, the ropes began to cut into the bollard. Our three-foot bollard was now a two-foot one. Since I was down, Mick had no choice but to follow.

On the Tongue, we found the Crumbs were forty feet high. Mick was feeling unwell, with both throat and general lassitude. Mists surged over our glacial peninsula. I guessed that we wanted to end up near the tip of the Tongue. But in the mist there was no horizon. I walked first, throwing snowballs ahead, while Mick followed, axe ready in case I walked over a cornice. When the snowballs disappeared without leaving a snowball-sized hole, we moved back a few yards and set up the tent. Sleep followed brew. The evening sun cleared the fog, the cloud sea retreated. The tent had been perfectly placed, just fifteen feet from the edge.

We would try looking over the nearest bit of edge to see if we could find the descent line. We had no dead men for snow belays, and so we dug a large hole in the soft plateau. I got as deep into the hole as possible, with the idea that if the cornice should collapse, I would be sufficiently stuck fast not to be catapulted after Mick. Mick gingerly stepped towards the edge, then got on his stomach and crawled towards it. It was an easy cornice, and he descended a few feet before coming back to the belay.

"Well?"

"You try."

A few minutes later I was looking over the edge of the cornice, and saw the Descent Spur snaking down to the

English-Allen Prominence. At last I could believe we were going to survive this climb. Already I began to debate the value of it all. What is the point of mountaineering? It seemed to me in that moment that the nature of the goal did not matter. We are driven to reach for goals, but we can learn no lessons from them. There is no pot of gold, only the rainbow.

"I suppose it's because we live in an achievement-orientated society," I said to Mick. He looked at me as if I had just announced I was stark staring mad.

In the tent we discussed our plans, should we get down safely. Over to the north I could see the Yengutz Har Pass. I decided that after a day's rest I would try to cross it with Phil and Bruce. Mick said that if we could get down the next day, he would walk out to Hoppar the next morning, take the jeep and bus to Gilgit the following day and hope to catch his plane to London from Islamabad on Sunday.

"Why the great rush?" I asked.

"Because it means by Monday the 16th I shall have parked those civil service shoes under that civil service desk and saved a whole week's annual leave, know what I mean, Vic?" (Tap-tap).

It was a very cold night. My sleeping bag was solid with lumps of ice. The tent was lined with hoar frost. Ice crystals showered us with each movement. Although it was my turn, I asked Mick to make the morning brew. Mick was really good in that way, he could turn on instant energy, get the job done immediately and no fuss. It took an hour to pull our boots on. Rolling up the tent was an ordeal, we had to stop every few seconds to warm up the finger tips. It was blowing slightly, and −25° C. But as soon as we clambered over the cornice, we were out of the wind.

Two abseils, leaving our precious Russian titanium icescrews behind, and the rest of the Spur was just a matter of ploughing down the waist-deep snow. The deep powder gave way to crust and, not learning from our experiences, we happily clanked and hobbled down the ridge. Iqbal, at Base Camp, was watching through binoculars. He could see us descending, and Phil and Bruce climbing up the Spur to help us down. At 9.00 am the morning sun had begun its work, and we stopped for suncream and the last Crunchy bar. The ridge had become hard, baked by the sun, like a pavement of ice. I should have recognised the signs. As we sat on our rucksacks, there was a characteristic 'oomph'.

"Did you hear that, Mick?"

"Yes, but there seem to be no signs or cracks here."

So we continued over the next rise, and there on the ridge below us were Phil and Bruce waving. We were about 200 yards apart. The slope between us had been stripped of its cover.

"Look what we've done!"

"Good lord."

"Clever, aren't we?"

I thought, as Bruce took Mick's rucksack and Phil took mine, that this was one act of kindness I should never forget. And at last here was someone else to talk with, someone whose recurrent topic of conversation was not about getting back to the office for Monday, even if that person was the best alpinist in the world.

Iqbal, Lobby, Bruce and I did eventually complete the traverse of the pass. It took us four hard days for the round trip, much longer than we anticipated. We made the mistake of selling our rope in Hispar, then descending the Hispar Gorge on the wrong bank, finding ourselves soloing across difficult rock-climbing ground above the roaring Hispar river. The other three showed great patience, waiting for me, tired and emaciated.

As for Mick, I don't know where he got the energy from, but he caught the flight. By Monday morning, 9.30 sharp, those civil service shoes were under that civil service desk.

APOLOGUE

The Globe, autumn 1987

Shuffle, stride, shuffle, run. It was enough to make me wheeze, but not bring on a full-scale asthma attack, a gentle trot, fifteen minutes, if that. That's the trouble with returning from expeditions, you are always so unfit. Trainers kicking through the damp leaves and spiky baubles – fruit of the Georgian plane, the absolute sign of a London autumn. A faint perfume of urea clung to the rotting leaves and baubles. Another sign of impending winter. I turned from the street and ran through the estate.

It was almost night. The last gasps of light were hanging from the base of the cloud table. Twilit towers, the glazed windows picked out in a bloody glow, were massed in ordered columns against the dark air; battery dwellings, insulated against the thin autumn chill.

And there at last was the inelegant Edwardian pile. Left, or at least left over, by the planners like an orphan on the corner of the tower block estate. Those depressingly unenlightened proportions, lurking like an ogre under the cover of dark. But it couldn't hide, the sheer bulk was always there. I paused, bathed in the sodium street glare, picking out the gilded letters over the door. G.L.O.B.E. From the bowels of that black carcass emanated the cacophony of jukebox and television locked in mortal conflict. My fist hammered on the door, it jarred open and spewed out a sheet of yellow light. In we go, I said.

Groping towards the bar, it was noisy and the glasses

immediately steamed over. The team was here, each at their favourite tipple, Lobby clutching a glass of real ale, John and Liz sipping gin and tonic, Mick quaffing cheapest bitter. Lobby produced a pouch of vile tobacco and offered me a roll-up. I was instructed to order another pint of cheapest. As usual, Lorrette took the order without breaking her simultaneous conversation. I wondered if she was bilingual, she would have made a fortune in Strasburg. Being Wednesday, we were treated to her lurex leopard-spot tights, with purple stilettos. Thursdays were always the gold lamé tiger stripes; her companion, my neighbour, a skinhead gorilla with tattooed arms the size of tree trunks, recognised us and landed a bear-sized slap on my shoulders.

"Aaargh," I wheezed back at him.

Lobby and Mick had grabbed seats under the television. I joined them, wedged in like a game of sardines. We grinned inanely at each other and raised the beer glasses. A magazine lay open on the table. It too was soaking in the beer. The picture showed a giant precipice festooned with séracs. Liverpool had just scored, so it was far too noisy to talk. But we tried anyway. I could just make out the words, sometimes.

" . . . unclimbed . . . "

" . . . and left . . . these séracs . . . "

" . . . four of us. Should be really good . . . "

I was conscious of a growing foreboding. Ripples of unease. These pub conversations. I really ought to have known better. But . . . and then again . . . and that picture . . .

INDEX

All Sphere Books are available at your bookshop or newsagent, or can be ordered from the following address:

Sphere Books,
Cash Sales Department,
P.O. Box 11,
Falmouth,
Cornwall TR10 9EN.

Alternatively you may fax your order to the above address. Fax No. 0326 76423.

Payments can be made as follows: Cheque, postal order (payable to Macdonald & Co (Publishers) Ltd) or by credit cards, Visa/Access. Do not send cash or currency. UK customers: please send a cheque or postal order (no currency), and allow 80p for postage and packing for the first book plus 20p for each additional book up to a maximum charge of £2.00.

B.F.P.O. customers please allow 80p for the first book plus 20p for each additional book.

Overseas customers including Ireland, please allow £1.50 for postage and packing for the first book, £1.00 for the second book and 30p for each additional book.

NAME (Block Letters) ....

ADDRESS ....

....

☐ I enclose my remittance for _____

☐ I wish to pay by Access/Visa Card

Number ☐☐☐☐☐☐☐☐☐☐☐☐☐☐☐☐

Card Expiry Date ☐☐☐☐

Brian 24/07/91